Creative
Destruction

Creative Destruction

An Introduction

John T. Dalton and Andrew J. Logan

CATO INSTITUTE
WASHINGTON, DC

Paperback ISBN: 978-1-952223-98-3
eBook ISBN: 978-1-952223-99-0

Printed in the United States of America.

CATO INSTITUTE
1000 Massachusetts Ave. NW
Washington, DC 20001
www.cato.org

CONTENTS

Introduction

What This Book Is About

This book is about "creative destruction," a term popularized by the Austrian economist Joseph Schumpeter. Creative destruction is used to describe change in the economy caused by innovations (the creation) and the effects of that change on the status quo (the destruction).

As our book will show, creative destruction is a force so powerful that it has shaped not only economies but also politics, culture, and social relations. Creative destruction sculpts the riverbed over which the waters of economic history flow, which is why it captured Schumpeter's imagination generations before the rise of Silicon Valley and the mantra of "disruption" reintroduced creative destruction to the public.

What This Book Covers

In contrast to Schumpeter's famously lengthy books (his *Business Cycles: A Theoretical, Historical, and Statistical Analysis of the Capitalist Process* exceeded 1,000 pages!), this book is substantially shorter. We focus solely on one of Schumpeter's key economic ideas—creative destruction—at a level that is informed by academic research but is intended to be accessible to a wide audience and not overly technical on the economics.

Readers of our book will gain a comprehensive understanding of creative destruction. They will learn the meaning of the concept, why it is important for economic growth, and how understanding its centrality influences our understanding of capitalism: what causes it, who initiates it, who resists it, and what its social, cultural, and political consequences are.

Who This Book Is For

Although Schumpeter was a gifted lecturer, his works were primarily written for an audience deeply familiar with the key economic terminology, thinkers, and concepts of his time. Our book aims to translate Schumpeter's ideas into a popular contemporary setting, reframing them in a manner accessible to any intelligent reader interested in the concept of creative destruction. Little background in economics is assumed, although we offer extensive citations for readers eager to delve into the rich literature surrounding creative destruction.

How This Book Is Structured

This book begins by answering the question of what creative destruction is, why the concept was so revolutionary for its time (and continues to be today!), and how Schumpeter's upbringing in the swirling, cosmopolitan melting pot of Vienna influenced his intellectual development that culminated in the theory. We transition to analyzing how creative destruction is intimately linked to economic growth and how viewing the economy as a ceaseless process of creative destruction influences our approach to several contemporary public policy questions.

Next, the book outlines the main cause of creative destruction—innovation—and how it can be either brought about or stopped. To expand on this point, we give two contemporary case studies of creative destruction: one where creative destruction was allowed to work and another where it was partially blocked because of fears about its cultural, social, and political consequences. We use this second case study as a natural bridge to explore the sociopolitical effects of creative destruction. We pay special attention to how creative destruction can become a victim of its own success and is often halted by policymakers fearful of disruptive technological change.

1

Schumpeter's Big Idea

The Music Industry and Creative Destruction

Music is astonishingly diverse. Twelve simple notes can be arranged in seemingly infinite ways to evoke thoughts, feelings, and memories. The instruments we use to play those notes are limited only by our imagination, which is why all of us—from shower singers to rock stars—are musicians of some kind. With such low barriers to entry, it is no wonder that new genres and artists spring up constantly with fresh, innovative sounds to serve every kind of taste.

The speed and intensity of innovation in music are matched perhaps only by how we consume it. In just over a century, Thomas Edison's humble phonograph has given way to streaming services like Spotify and Apple Music. In between came the radio, the record player, the cassette, the Sony

Walkman, the compact disc (CD), the virtual music library, and the iPod. Music is a dynamic, lively industry whose innovations reach not only our ears but also our politics, our economy, and our social development. These innovations have profound consequences. Just as the iPod swept away the market for CDs, American folk rock galvanized a generation that helped sweep away a political old guard dedicated to prosecuting the Vietnam War no matter what the cost.

Economics has a term that captures both the causes and effects of innovations like those in the music industry. That term is "creative destruction," a theory about what drives economic change in a capitalist economy. "Creative" refers to new innovations brought to market. "Destruction" refers to the fate of those antiquated products, processes, and social modes of organization that such innovations replace. Both halves of the term are expansive; examples of creation can range from thrash metal to the first record player or wireless headphones, whereas destruction can include not only direct economic effects, like the collapse in sales of cassettes after the advent of the CD, but also the social and political consequences of the innovation, such as the role played by new music in the protest movement against the Vietnam War. The term "creative destruction" endures among economists because it beautifully captures one of the most important insights in all of economics: that any action, in this case innovation, has its costs and benefits. Indeed, after Adam Smith's invisible hand, creative destruction might be the most cited concept in the glossary of economics terminology.

There is no single widely accepted statistic that economists use when measuring the extent and magnitude of creative destruction. In this book, we will use a variety of both quantitative and qualitative evidence in describing what creative destruction is and what the effects it unleashes are. We tend to rely more heavily on the qualitative evidence to make the book as accessible as possible. However, there are cases—the music industry being one—for which available quantitative data clearly demonstrate the presence of creative destruction.

Figure 1.1 presents data published by the Recording Industry Association of America (RIAA), a trade organization that represents the interests of the U.S. recording industry.[1] The data in Figure 1.1 show the changing demand for different media formats over the period 1973 to 2021.[2] The 8-track tape and vinyl record give way to the cassette, which gives way to the CD, which is finally overtaken by digital downloads— each format rising and falling in successive waves of creative

Figure 1.1
U.S. Recorded Music Sales Volumes by Format

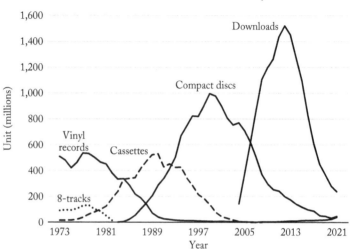

Source: Recording Industry Association of America database.

destruction coinciding with the introduction into the marketplace of new technologies for listening to music.

The collapse in digital downloads at the end of the period in Figure 1.1 occurs because the data are based on ownership by the consumer of the different formats, such as a collection of CDs or a library of songs on iTunes. Digital downloads, like the technologies before them, have largely been replaced by the latest wave of innovation—in this case, streaming music over the internet through such services as Spotify. The rise of streaming services can be seen in Figure 1.2, which shows the revenue associated with each format.[3] Like Figure 1.1, the waves of creative destruction can be clearly identified.

Although the data in Figures 1.1 and 1.2 clearly show examples of the economic effects of creative destruction in the music industry, they do not reveal the richness of the cultural, social, and (as in the case of the Vietnam War) political

Figure 1.2
U.S. Recorded Music Revenues by Format

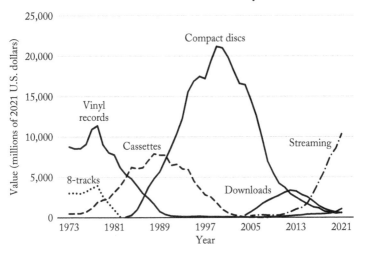

Source: Recording Industry Association of America database.

changes taking place, in part because of creative destruction in the music industry. Creative destruction is, at its heart, economic in nature, but its effects proliferate beyond the purely economic sphere. Our analysis of creative destruction throughout this book begins from an economic perspective but eventually expands to consider the wider field of cultural, social, and political effects.

We can explore the wider implications of creative destruction in the music industry by considering how the listening experience changed with various innovations. The way listeners interact with music has come to depend heavily on the format in which music is delivered. Cassettes did not allow for an unbroken listening session—for example, as the tapes needed to be flipped from one side to another to access the full content, say, of a music group's album. Cassettes were portable and relatively inexpensive, though, so music could be easily shared. Moreover, the tapes could be duplicated cheaply. The only equipment required to make copies was dual cassette decks, a feature widely available on home stereo equipment at the time. Copying tapes gave rise to the cultural phenomenon of mixtapes, that staple of romantic relationships in high school and beyond. Listening to music is one way we as humans feel, share, and express emotions with one another, so it is not surprising that mixtapes became so important during the era of cassettes. Listeners were no longer constrained by the decisions of artists and record studios about how to sequence songs on a tape. Instead, listeners could pick and choose songs from their stock of cassettes to design the perfect listening experience—one designed, for example, to express feelings to a high school sweetheart. Those mixtapes now mostly lie buried in landfills or are collecting dust in storage. But the legacy of mixtapes—the ability to create listening experiences designed by the listener—survives today in the form of the digital or streaming playlist.

Unlike cassettes, CDs allowed for one continuous listening session. Although there is now some doubt to the traditional story behind its creation, the CD is often said to have been designed by its creators Philips and Sony to play through the entirety of Beethoven's Ninth Symphony.[4] Whatever the true story behind the creation of the CD, the point remains the same: there are musical experiences enhanced by continuous playthroughs. CDs also allowed for rapidly clicking through to find specific tracks on a disc, which greatly alleviated the clumsiness of skipping undesirable songs on a cassette.

Although mixtapes represented the beginnings of a world in which listeners could control the sequencing of songs, the basic unit of distribution from artist to listeners remained the album throughout the era of CDs. It is true consumers could buy singles during this time, but even singles were packaged with other songs by the artist. This system would change with the innovation of digital downloads and then streaming.

Digital downloads and streaming completed the transition begun by mixtapes to a world in which listeners have the power to choose only the songs they desire to hear. Individual songs could be purchased through a service like iTunes or, later, streamed through a service like Spotify or YouTube. Although artists still create albums, listeners can pick and choose what they want to purchase and listen to. This mode of distribution breaks down the need for one continuous listening session, and thus it changes the incentives for artists in how they construct their albums by curating the selection and sequence of the songs on them.

Moreover, digital downloads ushered in a new era of copying in which artists and their record labels lost control over the sharing of their music. The result was a collapse in revenue from song and album sales. The music industry responded at the time by fighting the innovators of digital downloads, such as when the gods of the heavy metal genre, Metallica, sued Napster for copyright infringement. Napster was a peer-to-peer file-sharing network on which Metallica's songs were widely available and free for anyone to download as long as they had access to a computer, an internet connection, and Napster's software. Metallica and Napster agreed to a settlement. Although Napster would eventually be forced into bankruptcy, the wave of innovation and creative destruction the company came to symbolize would ultimately transform the music industry. Artists and recording studios adapted to the collapse in song and album revenues by relying more heavily on revenue from goods and services complementary to their songs and albums, such as live concerts.

The few examples we have discussed here are only some of the many and varied ways in which innovations in music delivery have led to cultural, social, and political effects due to creative destruction. To reemphasize the point, although creative destruction is typically economic in its origins, the effects of creative destruction can go beyond the purely economic realm to the cultural, social, and political realms as well. The music industry is a vivid example of how far-reaching the effects of creative destruction can be. Using the music industry as an example to introduce the idea of creative destruction has the additional benefit of music relating to most people's lives. Readers will recognize our examples as part of their own lives and experience. This suggests that viewing the economy through the lens of creative destruction will be a powerful analytical tool to help explain the changes we witness, especially if the example of the music industry is generalizable, which, as we will argue throughout the book, it surely is.

Indeed, if what is happening in the music industry is also happening across other industries and products, then we should be able to see the effects of creative destruction when looking at the economy at a macroeconomic level.

One direct economic effect of creative destruction occurs in the labor market—a job is created; a job is destroyed. As a result, an obvious place to look for evidence of creative destruction is the overall labor market. Figure 1.3 shows the job creation and job destruction rates for the U.S. economy from 1978 to 2020. The data are taken from the U.S. Census Bureau's Business Dynamics Statistics.[5]

The time series lines show the total number of jobs created and destroyed as a share of U.S. employment. The data show that creation and destruction in the labor market are regular features of the economy. Job creation typically outpaces job destruction, as we would expect in a vibrant economy growing over time. Job destruction is only higher than job creation in eight of the years in the sample, which coincided with periods of recession and economic crisis, like the subprime mortgage crisis of 2007 and 2008. The last thing to notice about

Figure 1.3
Jobs Created and Destroyed in the U.S. Labor Market

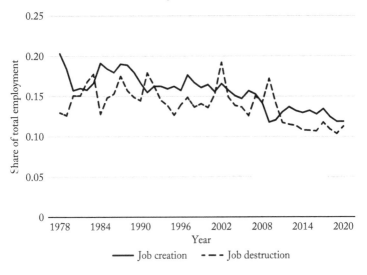

Source: U.S. Census Bureau, Business Dynamics Statistics website.

Figure 1.3 is that creative destruction in the U.S. labor market has been trending slightly downward in the last 20 years of the data. Fewer jobs are being created, and fewer jobs are being destroyed, both as a share of total employment. This is an indicator of declining dynamism in the labor market, a worrying trend for the state of creative destruction in the U.S. economy.

The clear evidence of creative destruction at the micro level (in the example of the music industry) and the macro level (in the example of the labor market) highlights the importance of creative destruction for understanding economic dynamics. There is, however, a greater argument: creative destruction is the *essential driving force* of capitalism. This is Schumpeter's Big Idea. To understand it, let us consider the man and economist, Joseph Schumpeter, and the society in which he grew up, Vienna.

Schumpeter and His Perennial Gale of Creative Destruction

The term "creative destruction" is first credited to the German economist and sociologist Werner Sombart, but it is more readily identified with the Austrian economist Joseph Schumpeter, who brought the term to prominence in 1942 in the book that is now considered his magnum opus, *Capitalism, Socialism and Democracy*. Schumpeter describes creative destruction as a process "of industrial mutation . . . that incessantly revolutionizes the economic structure from within, incessantly destroying the old one, incessantly creating a new one. This process of Creative Destruction is the essential fact about capitalism."[6] To Schumpeter, this "perennial gale of creative destruction" is central to capitalism and lies at the heart of innovation.[7]

Why the focus on innovation for understanding Schumpeter's gale? In directing his work here, Schumpeter was swimming against the dominant economic theories of the time. When he was writing in the early 20th century, economics relied on static analysis, an approach that studies an economy at a particular point in time, usually involving the notion of an equilibrium, or an economy at rest. This type of analysis is at the heart of most undergraduate economics curricula throughout the world even to this day, and with good reason. Static equilibrium analysis provides useful insights for understanding the determination of prices, how goods and services are allocated throughout the economy, why firms and households make the decisions they do, and many other ideas. What is missing, however, is a rich theory of economic dynamics. No innovation or technological change occurs.

In Schumpeter's time, economic growth was assumed to be the result of the steady, incremental accumulation of capital. It was Schumpeter who realized that such gradual wealth accumulation could not explain the explosion of economic growth and human prosperity unleashed by the Industrial Revolution and continuing into his own time, which the economist Deirdre McCloskey calls the "Great Enrichment."[8] Schumpeter's experience with economics can be described as a conflict of visions. The models were insufficient; they did not accurately describe the world as he saw it.

To Schumpeter, the Great Enrichment was better explained by the breakneck pace of innovation that characterized the 19th and 20th centuries. Mechanization, combustion engines, electricity, plumbing, chemicals, refrigeration—these innovations and more were responsible for the increasingly prosperous world in which Schumpeter grew up. This perspective influenced Schumpeter's view of the accepted economic theory of his day and led him to develop a theory of dynamics based on innovation. He shared his ideas with the world in 1911 with the publication of *The Theory of Economic Development*. In contrasting his view with the standard theory at the time, Schumpeter wrote: "Development in our sense is a distinct phenomenon, entirely foreign to what may be observed in the circular flow or in the tendency towards equilibrium. It is spontaneous and discontinuous change in the channels of the flow, disturbance of equilibrium, which forever alters and displaces the equilibrium state previously existing."[9]

Yet Schumpeter is hailed today as an economic prophet for his recognition of not only the benefits of innovation but also the tremendous societal disruption that comes with it. Schumpeter had an up-close and personal look at both the creation and destruction caused by innovation through his childhood upbringing in the swirling, cosmopolitan melting pot of Vienna in the twilight years of the Austro-Hungarian Empire. A brief historical tour of the Vienna of Schumpeter's time not only helps contextualize the origins of his vision of innovation and creative destruction, but also provides us with a glimpse of how the forces of creative destruction lead to a transforming society. We may recognize the dynamism of Schumpeter's Vienna in our own time and place, or we may recognize the absence of such dynamism and the missed opportunity that absence represents. Either way, the comparison is instructive.

Schumpeter was born in 1883 in the small Czech village of Triesch in the Austro-Hungarian Empire. At the age of four, his upper-middle-class upbringing was derailed when his father died. In pursuit of a better life for her son in Austria-Hungary's rigid, class-defined society, Schumpeter's mother, Johanna, moved with her son to the city of Graz, where she eventually remarried a noble military commander 30 years her senior. The marriage provided the social standing necessary to open the way for Schumpeter to pursue an elite education. In 1893, Johanna moved the Schumpeter family to Vienna, the capital of the Hapsburg Empire and one of the great intellectual centers of Europe.

There, Schumpeter attended the Theresianum, a rigorous preparatory school where his precociousness shone. Founded by the empress Maria Theresa in 1746, the Theresianum was generally open only to the sons of the nobility, including the stepsons of noble military officers. The school was considered the best in the Austro-Hungarian Empire, and Schumpeter received an outstanding education. At the Theresianum, Schumpeter acquired his lifelong appreciation of deep learning and knowledge. He spent much of his time there immersed in books, reading deeply beyond the standard curriculum, a practice he would continue throughout his life. Schumpeter's biographer Robert Loring Allen writes: "The Theresianum taught him that he could learn, that books and ideas were open to him, that much of life involved playing with these ideas. He learned there was no subject he could not conquer if he put his mind to it. He not only learned but learned how to learn."[10]

After graduating from the Theresianum, Schumpeter enrolled at the University of Vienna, which at the time was one of the world's best places to study economics. Under the tutelage of mentors like Eugen von Böhm-Bawerk, Schumpeter was exposed to competing theories of capitalism at a time when Vienna was industrializing, a process that ushered in a "techno-romantic" Vienna that would inspire Schumpeter's theory of creative destruction.[11] The term "techno-romantic" emphasizes the clash between technological change and capitalist society on the one hand and imperial and aristocratic society on the other, taking place in turn-of-the-century Vienna, the period in which Schumpeter grew up. By the time Schumpeter moved to Vienna as a young boy, the city had been the seat of power of the ruling Hapsburg dynasty for over 600 years.

The emperor at the time was Franz Joseph I. His authority, his court, and the aristocracy that was the base of his power were firmly entrenched in Viennese society and together ruled—albeit constrained as a constitutional monarchy—over vast stretches of territory in what is now Austria, Hungary, Czechia (formerly the Czech Republic), Slovakia, and other states. At the same time, technological change and the growth of capitalist society were creating new sources of political, social, artistic, and economic power backed by the emergence of such groups as the bourgeoisie, whom we would now call the middle class, and the urban poor.

The challenge for a ruling dynasty at the time, including that of Franz Joseph I, was to harness the benefits of technological and economic change to maintain its political position vis-à-vis other states and empires while simultaneously preventing those same technological and economic forces from curtailing or usurping its power domestically, either through reform or revolution. In the end, the defeats of World War I led to the collapse of the Austro-Hungarian Empire and the end of Hapsburg rule. Even if the Hapsburg dynasty had survived the war, and the Second World War after the First, it would not have emerged with the same power and influence as before, as the surviving monarchies in Europe to this day clearly attest. The transformations unleashed by the Industrial Revolution and the Great Enrichment were simply too great.

This period of immense social and economic transformation helps explain Schumpeter's focus on understanding economic dynamics. Indeed, economists would consider the period during which Schumpeter learned economics and began his career as an economist to coincide with one of the most consequential periods of creative destruction in all of human history. The creation was the birth of the modern world in the form of the Industrial Revolution; the destruction was the collapse of the feudal order. These events played out over a long period, but the shifting ground was evident for all to see, as the example of the Austro-Hungarian Empire suggests. Schumpeter was attuned to these macroeconomic changes not only as a scholar but also as a practitioner of economics. He briefly served as Austria's finance minister after World War I.[12] Below the surface of these tectonic economic changes, Schumpeter would have also observed the effects of creative destruction taking place on a much smaller scale, all around him, in his daily life in Vienna. He would later recognize that the accumulation of these changes is what incessantly revolutionizes the economic structure from within.

Probably the most oft-cited anecdote of Schumpeter's life was the joke he apparently used to tell. He claimed he wanted to be the greatest economist in the world, the greatest horseman in Austria, and the greatest lover in Vienna. The punch line was that he had only succeeded in two of the three, having never perfected his horsemanship. Although couched as a joke, the anecdote reveals Schumpeter's highly ambitious nature.

He was in the right city. For the budding social scientist trying to explain the world around him, Vienna would have been Schumpeter's laboratory, and his forays around the city his experiments. Indeed, Schumpeter's family apartment was situated only 100 feet from the imperial Parliament building along Vienna's Ringstrasse, a circular boulevard that wraps around the center of the city and is lined with key administrative buildings and works of monumental architecture, including city hall, the opera house and theater, multiple museums, elegant mansions, and the imperial palace, among others, sights that continue to convey the grandeur of imperial Vienna to residents and visitors to this day. Schumpeter biographer Thomas McCraw compares the location where

Schumpeter grew up to living next to the U.S. Capitol in Washington, DC, Parliament in London, or the Vatican in Rome and notes how Schumpeter would have absorbed lessons about architecture, art, and politics as he passed by daily.[13]

Moreover, the history of the Ringstrasse's development, which Schumpeter would have known well, was an example itself of creative destruction. The Ringstrasse perfectly encircles the center of Vienna; before its construction in the mid-19th century, walls and ramparts stood in its place to defend the city from potential invaders. The creation of a grand boulevard to showcase the wealth and power of the Hapsburg Empire necessitated the destruction of the old city walls. On one level, the Ringstrasse's development provides an example of creative destruction occurring not from innovation and market forces but from urban planners and government decree, in this case from Emperor Franz Joseph I. On a deeper level, however, it was innovations in cannon technology and military doctrine that rendered city walls obsolete, not just in Europe and Vienna but everywhere the latest technology in artillery was adopted and deployed. The creation of something so new in the Ringstrasse—with its modern administrative buildings and cultural institutions, wide boulevards to accommodate increased traffic demands, and streetcar lines—to replace something so old as the city walls—which had stood for about 600 years—would have made an impression on all who witnessed and experienced the effects of this act of creative destruction, including the young Schumpeter.

For longer excursions beyond the Ringstrasse, Schumpeter would have taken the city's Stadtbahn, or public railway system. The Stadtbahn was redesigned and expanded by the architect and urban planner Otto Wagner. Wagner worked primarily in the art nouveau style, which emphasizes curves and floral patterns, and his railway infrastructure—much of which remains in service in the modern Viennese public transit system—was an example of this new style. He mixed these elements with more traditional building styles and bathed the structures in distinctive white and green.

The Wagner railway system illustrates techno-romantic Vienna by the merger of old and new—traditional building styles mixed with art nouveau elements and coupled with the functionality of a modern transit system. Wagner's approach was intentional, as he later said he was trying to achieve "a harmonization of art and purpose" in the design of the system's stations, bridges, and other infrastructure.[14] Schumpeter would later identify this combination of existing resources to create something new as the main characteristic of his definition of innovation. The Wagner railway also illustrates another example of creative destruction, as old parts of the city were torn down to make room for the new and as rail replaced horse-drawn wagons and carriages.

A final example of how daily life in Vienna would have exposed Schumpeter to creative destruction is the arts. As the example of the music industry at the beginning of this chapter shows, innovation in artistic endeavors constantly remakes the cultural landscape in which we live. The Vienna of Schumpeter's time was no different, and even became renowned for its many famous artists and their impact on a range of fields, such as architecture, interior design, painting, music, and literature. Gustav Klimt, a painter, was one such artist. Over time, Klimt became one of Vienna's most famous artists, and his works, such as *The Kiss*, are recognizable to people around the world. The story of Klimt not only provides a glimpse at the cultural dynamics at work in techno-romantic Vienna but also illustrates the interconnecting parts of Schumpeter's theory of creative destruction, which is unleashed by entrepreneurs and other innovators.

Although Klimt is now famous for paintings such as *The Kiss*, he began his career as a more traditional artist. He painted in the prevailing styles on the murals in the Burgtheater, one of the new buildings along the Ringstrasse to showcase the cultural achievements within the empire. However, Klimt would not be bound by orthodoxy, and, as his style developed, he pushed artistic boundaries as far as he could. The cultural historian Carl Schorske writes, "Klimt was a questioner and a prober of the questionable, the problematical, in personal experience and in culture."[15] That included his more sexualized renditions of *Philosophy*, *Medicine*, and *Jurisprudence* commissioned by the University of Vienna, a building also located on the Ringstrasse. The response to his paintings would mark a turning point in Klimt's career. The outcry against his "pornography" was immediate. The paintings were not displayed, and Klimt refused public commissions for the rest of his life.[16]

Klimt's commission for the University of Vienna highlights the types of clashes taking place between innovators and the status quo in techno-romantic Vienna. Of course, he persevered and kept painting. Eventually, he would paint his "Golden Phase," including *The Kiss* and *Judith and the Head of Holofernes*.[17] Klimt's innovation was the combination of gold leaf with portraiture to create a new style forever associated with his name.

Klimt's struggles against the status quo as an artist and entrepreneur are emblematic, as Schumpeter would later argue, of what all agents of creative destruction—whether single entrepreneurs acting alone or larger groups of people working together in existing firms—face at one point or another. Creative destruction can be resisted. For creative destruction to be initiated by someone, the innovator must possess the psychological characteristics necessary to go against the prevailing tendencies in society, to break free of routine and risk condemnation to bring his or her vision of the world into reality. Klimt exhibited this type of courage, and so did many other people whose innovations unleashed creative destruction to make the Vienna of Schumpeter's time the beautiful chaos that it was.

One goal of this brief historical tour of techno-romantic Vienna has been to contextualize the origins of Schumpeter's vision of creative destruction. Vienna's history shows how creative destruction is not only economic, but also cultural and social. The Vienna of Schumpeter's time is exemplary of the extent and magnitude of the changes that societies can undergo because of creative destruction, but, of course, many places have undergone changes of similar extent and magnitude. The role of Schumpeter's genius in formulating his Big Idea of creative destruction cannot be ignored. Indeed, Schumpeter is widely considered one of the greatest and most original economic thinkers in all of history.[18] But the city of Vienna, more specifically the University of Vienna, still had one more role to play in understanding the development of

Schumpeter's ideas of creative destruction and, more broadly, how his education in economics positioned him to make such a fundamental contribution for understanding how capitalism evolves.

In short, Schumpeter's education as an economist bene-fited from his being in Vienna, which, with the University of Vienna leading the way, was one of the best places in all the world to study economics, second only to Great Britain. Carl Menger made fundamental contributions to economic theory, including his pioneering work on marginal utility analysis, that were remaking all of economics. Friedrich von Wieser and Böhm-Bawerk, who were both disciples of Menger's, built on Vienna's reputation for the study of economics.

It was Wieser who developed what became the standard term "marginal utility" to describe Menger's ideas. Wieser also made contributions to the study of what economists call "opportunity costs," the idea that in making a choice, the opportunity cost of that choice is the value of the next best choice not taken—that is, whatever has to be given up when making a choice. Böhm-Bawerk became famous for his work on interest rates and his critiques of Karl Marx.

Although Menger was not one of Schumpeter's teach-ers, both Wieser and Böhm-Bawerk were. These three economists—Menger, Wieser, and Böhm-Bawerk—would later be associated with what became known as the Austrian school of economics.[19] The economists F. A. Hayek and Ludwig von Mises would transplant the Austrian school to the United States, where it would continue to flourish in the post–World War II era.

Schumpeter's development as an economist benefited from the intellectual climate in Vienna and his proximity to so many influential economists. For example, he took Böhm-Bawerk's famous seminar class, which Mises also attended. Böhm-Bawerk's seminar was an extension of his scholarly interest in Karl Marx and became "a microcosm of the battles between socialism and liberalism, marginal utility and Marxist economics, and deductive and inductive social science."[20] Debating the ideas of Marx, which were all the rage at the time, with the other students, including Otto Bauer, Rudolf Hilferding, and Emil Lederer—all three devoted Marxists who would go on to their own distinguished careers—must have been an exhilarating experience for the young Schumpeter.[21] The experience certainly contributed to Schumpeter's great respect for Böhm-Bawerk. Schumpeter would eventually describe his old professor as a "great master" of economics, one Schumpeter was "sincerely and personally devoted to."[22] More importantly, Böhm-Bawerk's seminar, which ran from 1905 until 1914, became the testing ground for many of Schumpeter's early ideas. Schumpeter's own *The Theory of Economic Development* became one of the centerpieces of conversation during the latter part of the seminar's history.[23]

Marx's theories on the evolution of capitalism and the dynamics of history profoundly influenced Schumpeter, not because Schumpeter agreed with the mechanisms in Marx's theory, such as the accumulation of capital as the driver of economic growth, but because Schumpeter shared Marx's vision that the dynamics of capitalism were what mattered for explaining the evolution of markets, of history. Schumpeter jettisoned Marx's specifics for his own theory of innovation and creative destruction.

Schumpeter's classic *Capitalism, Socialism and Democracy*, in which he expounds on his theory of creative destruction, begins as an extended critique of Marx. Over the course of four chapters, Schumpeter considers Marx as a prophet, sociologist, economist, and teacher. The economist Ragnar Frisch once wrote to Schumpeter, "I have never met a person with your ability to and eagerness to understand the other fellow's point of view and to do him justice."[24] One imagines Schumpeter reliving his time in Böhm-Bawerk's seminar, sitting in the classroom in Vienna, perhaps gazing out the window onto the Ringstrasse as he collects his thoughts, thinking about how his early life and education shaped his vision of the world as he writes the opening chapters of his book.

The historical example of Schumpeter's Vienna and contemporary examples of the music industry or job churning in the U.S. labor market all illustrate the importance of creative destruction for understanding economic, cultural, social, and political change. They make clear why someone—student, economist, policymaker, voter—should care about understanding creative destruction. But as Schumpeter wrote, there is an even more important reason that creative destruction matters—its role in fostering economic growth. For it is economic growth that enables human flourishing along its many dimensions.

2

"It Is Hard to Think about Anything Else"

The Lucas Imperative

In the broadest terms, economic growth is defined as a sustained increase in the standard of living, whether at the global, country, county, city, or any other level. The most common way to measure economic growth is by changes in real gross domestic product (GDP) per capita. Real GDP is the total value of final goods and services produced in an economy during a particular period measured at a given price level. When economists speak about the size of an economy, or whether an economy grew or contracted over a given period, they are most often speaking about the level of or changes in real GDP. If real GDP is divided among all the people in an economy, then economists are speaking about real GDP per capita.

In measuring real GDP, economists think of the economy as a network of individuals occupying firms and households who are linked through their buying and selling. Depending on where real GDP is measured within this circular flow of the economy, the interpretation of real GDP changes. For example, economists often use the terms "real income per capita" or "real expenditure per capita" interchangeably with the term "real GDP per capita" because the total expenditure on all final goods and services within the circular flow—which measures real GDP—is equivalent to all the income earned within the circular flow. Real income per capita or real GDP per capita are most commonly used when discussing economic growth.

Real income per capita is an imperfect measure of the standard of living for two main reasons. First, real income per capita is an average and does not tell us anything about the distribution of real income within, say, a country. If two countries have the same level of real income per capita, one uniformly distributed and one highly unevenly distributed, then the standard of living will likely be lower for more people in the unequal case. Second, because it counts only economic goods traded for money, real GDP per capita does not account for economic "bads," like pollution from industrial production, which may negatively affect the standard of living, and it cannot measure the value of anything produced but not exchanged for money, like homemaking and caregiving for relatives.

These shortcomings of real GDP per capita are well known and have led some critics to propose alternative measurements of the standard of living—like gross national happiness—which are designed to account for more than just real income. Although these alternative measurements of standard of living may seem appealing, in practice they fail to improve much on real income per capita and are not widely used or likely to become widely used. Real income per capita remains the most relevant measure of the standard of living because real income is highly correlated with the good life. We need resources and income to purchase the things that matter to us, whether beer or soda for our movie nights at the theater or solar panels for cleaner energy.

Although modern economists track economic growth by measuring changes in real GDP per capita, the importance economists attach to economic growth for improving standards of living predates the development of GDP. Modern GDP statistics trace their origins only back to the 1940s.[1] Yet the question of economic growth has been central to the study of economics from the beginning, if by the "beginning" we mean the publication in 1776 of Adam Smith's *An Inquiry into the Nature and Causes of the Wealth of Nations*, the most commonly cited date for the birth of economics as a distinct field of study.

Why are some countries rich, and others poor? This is the ur-question in all of economics, and it runs through the heart of Smith's seminal treatise. Economists continue to seek new answers to many of the same questions that Smith explored in *The Wealth of Nations* even to this day. The reason so much scholarship has been devoted to this question is that economists believe the answers help us live better lives. Economists are often characterized as being cold-hearted rational thinkers, but many economists will tell you they became economists to help people. This is true historically and has been passed on as part of the lore of the profession. The great economist Alfred Marshall, for example, famously related how his tour of the slums, during which he looked upon the faces of the poor, moved him deeply. What he witnessed led him to pursue the study of economics as a way to improve the economic conditions he observed.[2] This strain of compassion throughout the history of economics is often ignored by the discipline's critics.

Yet the truth is that economics as a field of study arose from the idea that an understanding of the economy can be used to improve its functioning, which can improve all our standards of living, including the most disadvantaged among us. Adam Smith was a radical reformer fighting against the status quo of mercantilism, the system of political patronage characterizing the economy of his time. His arguments in *The Wealth of Nations* were persuasive; people were convinced that implementing Smith's ideas would spur economic growth and thereby help more people live better lives.

The work of economist Robert Lucas is a more recent example in the tradition of economists motivating the importance of achieving higher economic growth by highlighting growth's staggering effects on human welfare. Lucas, a longtime professor at the University of Chicago, won the Nobel Prize in Economics in 1995 for his contributions to macroeconomics. His 1988 paper "On the Mechanics of Economic Development" played a leading role in the emergence of so-called endogenous growth theory, the idea that the causes of long-run economic growth can be embedded within a mathematical model of the economy rather than rely on a change in external parameters of the model.[3] Lucas's insights helped shift the economics profession's focus away from business cycle analysis toward the question of what causes long-run economic growth.[4]

In Lucas's introduction to his paper, he describes his aims and motivations: "By the problem of economic development

I mean simply the problem of accounting for the observed pattern, across countries and across time, in levels and rates of growth of per capita income."[5] He then presents some facts related to these levels and rates of growth of per capita income. His data come from the World Bank's *World Development Report* of 1983.[6] Although the numbers today would be different, of course, and different countries may be involved, his point remains valid. The variation in the data across countries and time is striking in the extreme. For example, Lucas cites a 1980 average of $10,000 for per capita income for industrial economies, whereas India's is $240 and Haiti's is $270. The variation, Lucas writes, is "literally too great to be believed."[7] Next, he considers the variation across growth rates of per capita income, citing averages of 1.4 percent per year for India, 3.4 percent for Egypt, 7.0 percent for South Korea, 7.1 percent for Japan, and 2.3 percent for the United States during the two decades from 1960 to 1980. The cumulative effects of these differences over time lead to significant differences across countries. Indian income doubles every 50 years, whereas South Korean income doubles every 10 years. Or to frame it in more human terms, Lucas writes, "An Indian will, on average, be twice as well off as his grandfather; a Korean 32 times."[8] A life of grueling poverty versus the full participation in modernity and all the comforts it provides—these are the stakes. Lucas lays out the empirical case for why economists—for why *you*—should care about economic growth. He takes up the mantle passed on by Smith, Marshall, and many other economists throughout history as he builds up to his conclusion:

> I do not see how one can look at figures like these without seeing them as representing *possibilities*. Is there some action a government of India could take that would lead the Indian economy to grow like Indonesia's or Egypt's? If so, *what*, exactly? If not, what is it about the "nature of India" that makes it so? The consequences for human welfare involved in questions like these are simply staggering: Once one starts to think about them, it is hard to think about anything else.[9]

It is hard to think about anything else. Lucas's call to arms galvanized a generation of economists to renew the study of economic growth.[10] It reminds us what is at stake when economic growth slows down or speeds up. It also lays the groundwork for the moral case for trying to achieve higher economic growth (which we will return to later in this chapter) and indirectly explains why creative destruction matters. As we will soon see, creative destruction is a key driver or component of economic growth. Resistance to creative destruction will be a main theme throughout the latter part of this book. Keeping Lucas's point about the consequences for human welfare when economic growth—and thus creative destruction—slows down will remind us of why such a slowdown would be so costly and tragic for human lives.

Causes and Types of Economic Growth

So what causes economic growth? Lucas's paper considered the role played by the accumulation of human capital. Just as physical capital, like machines and structures, can be built up over time, economists speak of the accumulation of human capital in the form of education and learning by doing that increases a worker's productivity. Lucas showed that human capital better explains how economic growth occurs compared with previous theories based on physical capital accumulation and technological change. Of course, physical capital and technological change also contribute to economic growth. Tools are an example of physical capital that enhances worker productivity and can increase economic growth, whereas the mere existence of the tools is an example of technological progress.

As one might expect, economic growth has many different sources, which vary in the extent of their contributions to economic growth.[11] The division of labor matters. Multiple people working together can divide up the tasks required to complete a job and thus be much more productive than a single person responsible for all the tasks. International trade contributes to growth by allowing countries to specialize along the lines of their comparative advantage—for example, France producing and trading wine in exchange for Canadian lumber. Access to well-functioning credit markets can be important. If you have an idea for the next Big Thing that will revolutionize the economy but lack the financial resources to bring that idea to the market, then the idea enters the world stillborn. In explaining economic growth, many economists assign a prominent role to the quality of institutions—the rules of the game influencing the behavior of market participants.

Institutions can be both informal, like norms of social behavior, and formal, like a well-functioning court system for resolving disputes. Government policy frequently falls under the category of institutions. Liberalization policies, like reducing taxation and burdensome regulations, can spur economic growth. India experienced an explosion in economic growth in the years since Lucas used the country India as an example of low per capita income and sluggish growth. India's explosive growth was largely a result of reforms initiated in the 1990s that were designed to liberalize parts of the Indian economy.[12]

A more recent and prominent argument for what causes economic growth has been put forth by the economist Deirdre McCloskey. She argues that liberty and dignity are necessary for ordinary people—for you and me—to have a go, test their wares in the market, reap the benefits of their efforts, and be afforded dignity for such bourgeois peddling. Thus, it is liberty and dignity that unleashed the human creativity required to pull us out of the Malthusian world and into one characterized by sustained economic growth.[13] "Malthusian" refers to the early economist Thomas Robert Malthus, who lived from 1766 to 1834. Malthus theorized that as populations grew, agricultural output would be unable to meet the increased food demands and, thus, stagnation, poverty, and death would persist. The rapid—and still ongoing—increase in economic growth and food production that began in the 19th century proved Malthus spectacularly wrong. The title of McCloskey's book, coauthored with the economist Art Carden, summarizes the argument succinctly: *Leave Me Alone and I'll Make You Rich.*[14]

Although we have just described many different causes of growth, economists will sometimes divide economic growth into two categories: "Smithian" and "Schumpeterian." Smithian refers to Adam Smith and is meant to invoke core ideas from *The Wealth of Nations.* This type of growth stems from exchange and cooperation, such as the division of labor in Smith's now-famous example of the pin factory. International trade can be another example of Smithian growth, as international trade spreads the division of labor across national borders. Insofar as institutions facilitate exchange and cooperation, they would also be considered Smithian.

Of course, Schumpeterian growth is named after the same Joseph Schumpeter we encountered in Chapter 1. This type of growth comes from innovation or technological change. The evolution of the music industry from cassettes to compact discs to digital downloads and streaming is Schumpeterian. Although both Smithian and Schumpeterian growth may result in creative destruction, creative destruction is more commonly associated with innovation and technological change, hence "Schumpeterian."

Introducing this category of Schumpeterian growth now brings us to the crucial link between economic growth and creative destruction. Notice that sustained economic growth, independent of its causes, frequently requires creative destruction, especially over longer periods. Something new must be created to expand the economy, and the new creation displaces or destroys the old ways of being. It is hard to observe economic growth over long periods without also observing creative destruction. Anecdotally, we all know this to be true.

Well, "we" who live in places experiencing modern economic growth know so. We simply observe the world around us and see how it changes as we go through life, from corded telephones to wireless cellphones and sleek smartphones. In this way, creative destruction is a key driver of economic growth. As such, if society wants to promote economic growth as a goal, then society must also live with creative destruction. Economic growth and creative destruction come as a package deal.

Should economic growth be a goal of society? The data from Lucas's introduction give us a glimpse at the pragmatic case suggesting yes. All else equal, it is better for people to have higher rather than lower real incomes, especially in the case of relieving extreme absolute poverty. This is true even if relative poverty, in the form of greater income inequality, persists with higher economic growth. Let us further consider the pragmatic case for economic growth and then turn to the moral arguments for why economic growth and creative destruction promote human flourishing. In doing so, we will strengthen the case for letting creative destruction take place.

The Hockey Stick of Economic Growth

Economic growth and creative destruction built the modern world. Figure 2.1 shows the level of world real GDP per capita over the years 1 (CE) through 2008.[15] The y-axis is labeled

Figure 2.1
World Real GDP per Capita

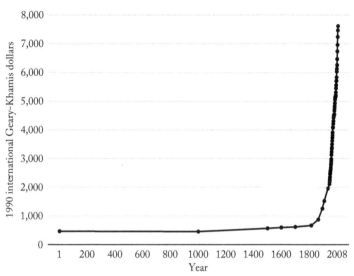

Source: Angus Maddison, "Historical Statistics of the World Economy: 1–2008 AD," 2010.
Note: GDP = gross domestic product.

in 1990 international, or Geary-Khamis, dollars. Geary-Khamis dollars were developed by the economic statisticians Roy C. Geary and Salem Hanna Khamis to make comparisons across countries and across time, and economists frequently use them to construct long-run growth pictures like that in Figure 2.1. They are designed to have the same purchasing power parity that the U.S. dollar did in the year 1990.

Purchasing power parity is a way to measure prices of specific goods across countries to compare living standards more accurately. The purchasing power of $100 in the United States today is very different from $100 in, say, Chad, because the basket of goods available to consumers in the two countries can differ substantially. Purchasing power parity adjustments make sure that the basket of goods is the same to properly compare what $100 can buy in the United States or Chad. The most famous example of purchasing power parity nowadays is the so-called Big Mac Index, which is published by *The Economist*.[16] The Big Mac Index is based on the clever idea that the McDonald's burger is relatively similar across countries, so that comparing its price reveals the purchasing power of local currencies relative to the U.S. dollar.

Each point on the line in Figure 2.1 represents an estimate of global real GDP per capita. Naturally, there are fewer points for most of the years compared with the last two centuries of data. But what estimates are available—along with the vast written scholarship of economic historians—paints a clear and dramatic picture: real income per capita for the world remains mostly stagnant throughout human history until something shocking—the Industrial Revolution—happens in the late 18th and early 19th centuries and real income per capita subsequently explodes. The picture of real GDP per capita for the world can be thought of as one long handle of a hockey stick on its side with the blade stretching out toward the end.

Three distinct phases are evident along the hockey stick. The period of stagnation corresponding with the handle represents what we have previously referred to in this chapter as the Malthusian world, as life for most of humanity resembled Malthus's vision of stagnation and poverty. Ironically, Malthus was living and writing in England during a time in which the Industrial Revolution was changing the world from one of stagnation to growth, but he failed to recognize the implications of what was happening in the economy around him. Technological improvements increased agricultural productivity high enough to meet the new demands on the food supply. Malthus's vision of the world remains influential to this day, especially among environmentalists and those concerned with global hunger who continue to believe that humanity's future is destined for stagnation when faced with increased population and economic growth and the inherent limitations of the earth's resources.

The second distinct phase of the hockey stick—the bend between the handle and the blade—is the period of transition between the Malthusian world and modernity, sparked by the Industrial Revolution. Many of the explanations for why the

Industrial Revolution emerged in Great Britain are similar to explanations of the causes of economic growth previously mentioned. The third distinct phase of the hockey stick, the blade, is what we call the modern world, or the period of modern economic growth, or as the economist Deirdre McCloskey prefers, the "Great Enrichment." Increasingly, economists are recognizing that the key fact of Figure 2.1 is not necessarily the Industrial Revolution, which ignited the fire of economic growth, but the *resilience* of that fire, which continues to burn in the form of the Great Enrichment. It is the Great Enrichment that built the modern world.

The magnitude of the change in the world's real GDP per capita represented by the data in Figure 2.1 is striking. From the year 1 to 2008, world real GDP per capita grows by approximately 1,530 percent. If we take the year 1700, the latest year in the data available before the Industrial Revolution, as a dividing line between the Malthusian world and the Great Enrichment, then world real GDP per capita increases by merely 24 percent between the years 1 and 1700. With regard to real GDP per capita, most of life before 1700 was the same. From 1700 to 2008, however, world real GDP per capita increases by nearly 1,140 percent. Although these numbers are big and the image in Figure 2.1 is striking, they do not fully reveal the true power of modern economic growth and creative destruction to increase living standards. The reason is that Figure 2.1 considers the world as a whole—the United States and Chad together, for example.

Figure 2.2 presents the same data of real GDP per capita broken down for the United States and various regions around the world.[17] As expected, over the last 100 years, the United States is the richest region with regard to real GDP

Figure 2.2
Real GDP per Capita around the World

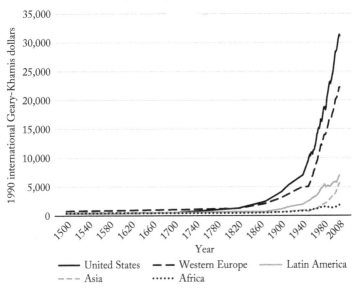

Source: Angus Maddison, "Historical Statistics of the World Economy: 1–2008 AD," 2010.
Note: GDP = gross domestic product.

per capita, followed by western Europe, Latin America, Asia, and then Africa. We are now dealing with the truly awesome numbers unleashed by the Industrial Revolution and sustained by the Great Enrichment.

From years 1 to 2008, U.S. real GDP per capita grows by 7,700 percent. Before the Industrial Revolution, from 1 to 1700, U.S. real GDP per capita increases by only 24 percent. Notice that before the Industrial Revolution this means the United States was just like the rest of the world, which, as we have seen, also grew by 24 percent over this period.[18] From 1700 to 2008, however, U.S. real GDP per capita grows by approximately 5,820 percent. Awesome. U.S. real GDP per capita did not double. It did not triple or increase tenfold. U.S. real GDP per capita increased by a factor of 78 from 1 to 2008. When faced with such magnitudes, *it is hard to think about anything else.*

That same passage from Lucas's paper began by imploring the reader to look at numbers like these as representing possibilities. The United States may be the richest region in Figure 2.2, but wherever economic growth and creative destruction have been unleashed, they have resulted in changes in real GDP per capita that have radically changed people's lives for the better. From Italy, Germany, and France in western Europe, to Canada and Australia, to Chile in South America, to Japan and the Asian Tigers, to the coastal regions of China, to many other places around the world, wherever modern economic growth emerges, lives are enriched and humans flourish. The Malthusian world becomes a distant memory.

Yet Figure 2.2 shows the possibilities for more economic growth around the world. Africa is the poorest region represented in the 2008 data in Figure 2.2. African real GDP per capita increased approximately 323 percent from 1700 to 2008, which is less than the change for the world (1,140 percent) and far below that in the United States (5,820 percent). Many people in Africa still live in the Malthusian world. Imagine the possibilities once economic growth becomes widespread in Africa. With over a billion people in Africa in the year 2021, imagine the possibilities for human creativity, whether in the arts, science, and technology, or new forms of organization.[19] Economic growth around the world is not zero sum—it can happen not only anywhere and everywhere, but wherever growth originates, and the rest of the world also benefits from the new ideas and products driving that growth.

Unfortunately, Africa also reminds us not to take economic growth for granted. It may seem obvious to readers living in places experiencing economic growth and creative destruction that these forces are good overall and that they will continue to improve our lives. But by taking them for granted, we risk lulling ourselves into complacency, dulling our senses to the threats undermining economic growth and creative destruction, and sapping us of our dynamism.[20] Whether our apathy toward economic growth results in policies restraining growth and creative destruction through the ballot box or changes in our individual behaviors and ambitions, the results can be the same. Economic growth can slow. It can stop. Argentina, for example, experienced rapid economic growth in the late 19th and early 20th centuries to become a relatively rich economy. That period was followed, however, by poor public policy decisions that contributed to slow and uneven growth for much of the rest of the 20th century so that Argentina's economic dynamism steadily declined.

Japan experienced its own so-called Lost Decade during the 1990s after real estate and other asset markets collapsed. Japan's Lost Decade continues to haunt policymakers around the world, as countries try to avoid Japan's fate. The term "Lost Decade" masks a graver threat, though, because Japan continues to experience sluggish growth. The more appropriate term right now would be the "Lost Three Decades and

Counting." Although the public policies have not been the same, the fear is that Japan seems to be similar to Argentina of the 21st century with regard to its sluggish growth experience relative to its prior dynamism.

And, of course, the U.S. economy has been underperforming since the onset of the Great Recession in 2007 and 2008. Much has been written about this "Great Stagnation."[21] Indeed, one of our own motivations for writing this book is to call attention to the role played by creative destruction in fostering growth and improving people's lives. The world needs more, not less, creative destruction and economic growth.

The Moral Case for Economic Growth

Schumpeter understood well the pragmatic case in favor of capitalism and the power of its essential driving force, creative destruction. *Capitalism, Socialism and Democracy* was first published in 1942, and subsequent editions appeared until 1950. Schumpeter was writing at a time when capitalism was under severe threat from economic depression and world war, so he was keen to remind readers about the positive case for capitalism. Schumpeter spends much of the chapter titled "The Rate of Increase of Total Output" going through some calculations and data similar in spirit to what Lucas did in his paper and what we have shown in Figures 2.1 and 2.2. He then points out how this growth mostly benefits poor households, as mass production brings once unimaginable goods within their budgets. The rich surely benefit from the introduction of new and cheaper goods, but their relative income and wealth is such that the marginal benefit to them is less than the poor receive. In what became a famous passage from *Capitalism, Socialism and Democracy*, Schumpeter writes, "The capitalist achievement does not typically consist in providing more silk stockings for queens but in bringing them within the reach of factory girls in return for steadily decreasing amounts of effort."[22]

Schumpeter sets up the case that capitalism, with its creative destruction and economic growth, increases human welfare. His argument for the positive effect on human welfare culminates in the chapter titled "The Civilization of Capitalism," in which he expands beyond the narrow empirical case to consider how life and civilization have been enhanced, or made possible, by capitalism, creative destruction, and economic growth.

Capitalism develops the use and practice of rational thought and "adds a new edge" to rationality in two interconnected ways.[23] The first is through how money becomes a unit of account used in cost–benefit calculations. Schumpeter cites the development of double-entry bookkeeping as an achievement along the road to capitalism, but his larger point is that the logic, attitude, or method of cost–benefit calculations begins to pervade all aspects of life, leading to advances across different fields. He cites the development of applied mathematics alongside the rise of capitalism as an example. This way of thinking is crucial for new enterprise and innovation.

The second way is how capitalism provides "the men and the means."[24] What Schumpeter means by this is that, as economic growth and creative destruction begin to release people from their Malthusian chains, they begin to spend their time and·resources innovating. As we pointed out in Chapter 1, the feudal order in Europe was brought down by an act of creative destruction. That opened many different pathways to success through economic means, not just the traditional justifications of the sword and the cross.

The growth in rational science and innovation fuels economic growth and transforms the world. The list is as long as we want to make it: steam engines, railroads, machine tools, silk stockings worn by factory girls, automobiles, antibiotics, airplanes, telephones and smartphones, the internet,

Google, and life-saving vaccines. But Schumpeter goes further than just the products we consume. Individualist democracy arises from capitalism as well, as more voices than just those of priests and kings demand a say in determining how society is run, commensurate with their new economic and social standing.[25] Economic growth even provides the greater means for social legislation—as the economy grows, redistributionist policies become relatively more affordable.

In summary, Schumpeter's description of capitalism's history takes us through the pragmatic case for economic growth up to the moral case. Economic growth and creative destruction represent Lucas's possibilities. Economic growth provides options now and in the future. It is how we create all those things we value most.

Should economic growth and creative destruction be a goal of society? Yes, emphatically yes. We have a moral obligation to ourselves, and to our posterity and others, to foster economic growth the best we can. The ability of the poorest among us, both close to home and around the world, to achieve better lives depends on it. And many such other possibilities—from life-saving cancer treatments to our children's future job prospects—depend on it. Indeed, most of those possibilities remain unknown to us, given our limited vision of the future.

The economist Tyler Cowen takes up this moral case for economic growth in his book *Stubborn Attachments*. The opening summary begins as follows:

> **Growth is good.** Through history, economic growth in particular has alleviated human misery, improved human happiness and opportunity, and lengthened human lives. Wealthier societies are more stable, offer better living standards, produce better medicines, and ensure greater autonomy, greater fulfillment, and more sources of fun. If we want to sustain our trends of growth, and the overwhelmingly positive outcomes for societies that come with it, every individual must become more concerned with the welfare of those around us.[26]

Cowen, echoing Lucas's call to arms, is taking up the mantle of Smith, Marshall, and Lucas. *It is hard to think about anything else.*

3

A Vision for a
Dynamic World

Creative Destruction Changes Our
View of Capitalism

Creative destruction is the essential driving force of capitalism. It brings capitalism to life, transforming it from a staid word endlessly bounced about by cable news pundits and college term papers into a concrete process whose effects we can see in everyday life. Not just the latest technological gizmos, creative destruction is the shuttering of the dry cleaners down the street thanks to a new door-delivery service. Creative destruction is the merger of two rival companies. Creative destruction abounds in art, music, and culture. Simply put, creative destruction unleashes change—unlocked by new ideas, sometimes backed by investors and implemented by innovators. Such change is often bumpy as it disrupts the jobs and the practices and norms of the status quo, but it is worthwhile in the long run, as the Great Enrichment demonstrates.

Understanding how central the creative destruction process is to capitalism has important implications for how we judge capitalism's performance. Joseph Schumpeter paints us a picture of a dynamic world that remains bitingly relevant to enduring—and recurring—criticisms of capitalism: inequality, the cruelty of economic downturns, and monopoly power. All of these and more are discussed in this chapter, which shows how recognizing the dynamism of capitalism offers three key insights. The first insight is that capitalism should be judged over time. The second is that we should judge capitalism not on the current state of the economic and social structure but rather on how that structure is created and destroyed. The third insight deals with the importance of competition as a result of innovation. We consider each in turn.

Before we do so, however, it is worth discussing what we mean by "judging" capitalism. Schumpeter himself uses the term in *Capitalism, Socialism and Democracy* because he was writing at a time when many thought the capitalist system stood on much shakier intellectual ground.[1] Not only was capitalism a comparatively young economic system, but the Soviet experiment was in full swing and the capitalist Western democracies were being threatened militarily by the Axis powers. Still raging was the so-called socialist calculation debate triggered in large part by the writings of the economist Ludwig von Mises.[2] The socialist calculation debate centered on the question of whether a centrally planned economy could properly compute the demand for goods and services, how to produce them, and how to allocate them without the invisible hand of prices and markets. To Schumpeter, all readers of his book in this fraught time were "judges" of capitalism, rendering their verdict around the family dinner table, in the seminar room, at the street protest, and at the ballot box, which ultimately influenced the level of state intervention in the economy. Although capitalism ended up dominating much of the second half of the 20th century, readers of this book are judges of capitalism as well. How we should design and govern our institutions and how much government intervention we would like in the economy are questions no less relevant for readers today than they were for readers in Schumpeter's own time.

Focus on the Long Run

The first insight into how we should judge capitalism considering creative destruction is that the economy should be judged primarily by its long-run performance. Creative destruction does not happen overnight, and its fruits take time to ripen. As we discuss in detail in Chapter 4, creative destruction requires that innovators wrangle together existing resources and new ideas and bring the resulting innovations to market all while battling the many obstacles to entrepreneurship. This is a slow-going process! Even slower is the destruction piece. Most status quo firms threatened by innovation do not go down without a fight. Incumbents will pull all sorts of levers—regulatory battles, new product releases, attempted buyouts—to forestall or halt creative destruction. Patience is the name of the game for innovators, just as it should be for critics of capitalism.

In light of this, capitalism should be evaluated by its long-term outcomes, not by its short-term inefficiencies. The Great Enrichment offers a prime example. Consider the time series we showed in Chapter 2: the hockey stick of economic growth. When we zoom in on that impressive feat, we find that the hockey stick is not as smooth as it appears, having plenty of bends, dips, and ridges. Behind that enormous increase in the standard of living are all sorts of negative shocks: recessions, depressions, high inflation, and periods of unemployment. Although the long-run increase is tremendous, any given snapshot of time is quite bumpy. When faced with these small snapshots of bumpy economic performance, critics of capitalism become indignant, and rightly so. "Why does capitalism produce such immiseration?" a critic might exclaim. "What if we could enjoy growth without the growing pains?" Deirdre McCloskey's Bourgeois Deal offers an answer.[3] In so many words: "Let people have a go. Let them innovate. Let them reap the rewards of their innovation. In the meantime, they will become fabulously rich, and inequality will emerge. But, over time, we will all become fabulously rich as innovation fuels economic growth."[4] The focus is rightly on the long term, because what ultimately matters are increases in standards of living, which are fueled by economic growth.

In addition, economists point out that recessions can contain silver linings. Here is where the brilliance of creative destruction shines. Schumpeter recognized that capitalism's inability to fully use all its resources at every point in time is one of the preconditions for its superior long-run economic performance. Put another way, the bumps and ridges on the hockey stick are among the forces that enable it to bend upward, delivering the massive economic growth that characterizes the Great Enrichment. The cause is creative destruction. Change, through destruction, clears the way to reap the benefits of creation. This destruction is costly in the short term. Workers lose their jobs and capital is lost as the economy slacks below potential, creating the bumps along the hockey stick. Yet business failures today free up the resources, labor, time, and capital needed for the successes of tomorrow. If the economy were always humming along at full throttle, there would be no room for creative destruction—no available capital for productivity-enhancing innovations, no labor to work the innovations, and no possibility for incumbents to be destroyed to make way for the innovations.[5]

The ebbs and flows of the business cycle under capitalism reflect this. The reason is that the volatility of the business cycle can be both a symptom of and a mechanism by which the creative destruction process works. Economic downturns in part enable creative destruction to work its growth-producing magic. Recessions increase the pace of labor reallocation because of a lower opportunity cost of such activities.[6] Economic downturns also reduce the opportunity cost of investing in new capital or reorganizing an industry, which in boom times would be disruptive for current production. Collectively, these effects turn an event that at first appears to be wholly negative—a recession—into one that can boost productivity and economic growth in the long run, contributing to keeping the Great Enrichment going. If we focus only on the negative aspects of recessions, we lose sight of the fact that recessions can be sources of capitalism's success through their contributions to reallocating resources and enabling future creative destruction and economic growth.

Focus on How Existing Structures Are Created and Destroyed

The second insight into how we should judge capitalism in light of creative destruction is that we should focus on how readily the social and economic structure changes rather than on the state of the structure at any given point in time. In Schumpeter's words, "The problem that is usually being visualized is how capitalism administers existing structures, whereas the relevant problem is how it creates and destroys them."[7] Put differently, policymakers and voters alike should focus less on how things are right now and more on the speed and direction at which change—embodied by creative destruction—is occurring. What does this look like in practice? Several examples help illustrate the point.

First is a historical example about regulation and oligopoly power from Schumpeter's own time. In *Capitalism, Socialism and Democracy*, Schumpeter was heavily critical of economists who called for stricter regulations on oligopolies—industries consisting of a few large firms that often collude to restrict output, keeping prices artificially high for consumers. To Schumpeter, oligopolistic arrangements did not necessarily result from producers plotting to rob consumer surplus, but from incumbent firms reacting to the rapid pace of creative destruction that characterized the early 20th-century U.S. economy. With relentless innovation across many industries, including energy, refrigeration, transportation, and lighting, Schumpeter argued that incumbents were colluding to wrestle away what profits they could before the ground shifted once more, rendering existing technologies and business models obsolete and destroying the incumbent oligopolists. Regulators focused on how the economic system looked during that snapshot in time—an oligopoly—without looking at the forces of change that would both lead to the status quo and transform it. As a result, Schumpeter thought that attempts to regulate oligopolies would slow creative destruction. Without the ability to earn high profits, innovators would have fewer incentives to pursue risky innovations. The result is that the pace of innovation—and thus creative destruction—would falter, ironically helping secure the very incumbent firms the regulatory action sought to undermine. Framing the concern over oligopoly in relation to creative destruction shifts the emphasis away from regulation to ensuring that conditions allowing entry by new competitors are preserved.

Moreover, regulating incumbents can worsen what economists refer to as rent seeking and regulatory capture. Rent seeking is when a firm engages in otherwise unproductive activities designed to increase its profits. The classic example is lobbying government officials to make regulatory changes that would be favorable to the firm doing the lobbying, and unfavorable to competitors. When regulations are created, such as those governing an oligopoly, they create incentives for firms to lobby for and manipulate those regulations. Economists consider rent seeking inefficient and harmful to society because resources are shifted away from productive activities, like innovation, toward rent seeking. Once regulations over firms are established, they can often lead to what economists call regulatory capture. Who might a firm like to hire to navigate the regulatory regime and lobby for changes in its favor? The regulators themselves make for prime targets for hiring, because, as the ones writing the regulations, they are naturally placed to navigate them and lobby for changes. Likewise, lobbyists for the firm are prime candidates for regulatory jobs, as they also know the ins and outs of the regulatory regime. In this way, regulatory regimes can create revolving doors between government officials and private-sector firms, which in practice often results in the regulations benefiting the lobbyists and regulators at the expense of society as a whole.

Second are the debates today around income inequality. In these debates, the main question considered is often whether the distribution of income in this generation is equal enough. An emphasis on creative destruction reframes this question. Creative destruction describes change as the essential fact of capitalism, so the question to consider regarding creative destruction and inequality is how income distribution changes over time. Is there social mobility? Do people at the bottom of the income distribution have the opportunity to advance upward? What about their children? At any given point in time, some inequality is to be expected, but in an economy properly characterized by creative destruction, those who occupy the various rungs of the income ladder should see their fortunes change either in their own lifetime or their children's lifetimes as Schumpeter's gale blows. Shifting the focus away from the extent to which the existing income distribution is unequal toward whether and how much people can move up and down that distribution is a more appropriate way of determining whether capitalism is "succeeding." Moreover, just as the mere fact of social mobility does not preclude redistribution being justified, the mere fact of present inequality does not require it.

Framing income inequality in relation to creative destruction has important policy implications. Creative destruction suggests that the typical response to income inequality in the form of higher taxation for high-income earners misses the mark, as it taxes upward mobility along the distribution. When politicians argue for taxing the rich to eliminate inequality, they frequently try to build support for such policies by casting rich people as exploiters living at the expense of the poorer masses. Yet populist rhetoric and policies designed to soak the rich often backfire, because they disincentivize upward mobility along the distribution, drive the rich to lobby for loopholes, and, in general, create conflict between income groups. This frequently happens for various reasons, such as elite entrenchment through government protection. Government protection could be rolled back to increase upward mobility. And policies can be designed to achieve greater equality by making it easier for people to climb the income ladder (rather than leveling by pulling some of them down), such as by expanding credit markets to young people to help finance their educations. The point of this discussion on inequality is not to suggest the optimal policy solution but rather the optimal framing with regard to creative destruction.

Third is the common accusation leveled against capitalism that it produces fraudulent actors. By this line of argumentation, the history of capitalism is ripe with rogues, swindlers, and frauds, and the existence of those bad apples is an indictment of the entire capitalist system.[8] That criticism misses two important points. The first is simply that fraudulent behavior is an inevitable fact of life in social interactions between flawed humans. Fraud exists in all societies, be they socialist or capitalist. The second is that capitalism possesses one of the best mechanisms for disciplining fraudulent actors—creative destruction. Proponents of this perspective focus excessively on the existence of bad apples in the present moment, ignoring how the dynamism of capitalism and the free entry and exit of firms that characterize creative destruction act to flush fraud from the economy.[9]

Whereas creative destruction is a mechanism by which capitalist societies can naturally police fraudulent behavior, the broader point that critics of capitalism miss is that capitalist societies tend to promote virtuous behavior on the whole. Market activity is based on exchange. We buy from the local bakery not because the baker *coerces* us to buy bread but because the baker *persuades* us to try the latest creation amid the aromas of loaves fresh from the oven wafting under our noses. "Please, try this fresh loaf of delicious bread. It will make your sandwich taste so much better." And the baker says it with a smile. Interacting with strangers in the market brings forth what McCloskey calls the "bourgeois virtues."[10]

Far from increasing fraud, capitalism promotes better behavior toward others. That market activity promotes virtue is actually an old argument in favor of capitalist societies.[11] Montesquieu wrote, "Commerce is a cure for the most destructive prejudices; for it is almost a general rule, that wherever we find agreeable manners, there commerce flourishes; and that wherever there is commerce, there we meet with agreeable manners."[12] Similarly, Voltaire wrote of the civilizing effects of the London stock exchange, as people from diverse religious backgrounds cooperated contently in their shared pursuit of riches.[13] More recent research confirms what thinkers like Montesquieu and Voltaire observed. Market economies improve trust, cooperation, and moral behavior toward others.[14]

A better way of viewing the problem of fraud is to recognize that creative destruction is the sword of Damocles hanging over the necks of potentially fraudulent economic actors—often deterring fraud before it happens. Imagine that a firm commits fraudulent behavior, such as a local car repair shop's mechanics repeatedly "finding" new problems with their customers' cars unrelated to the service call at hand and recommending expensive repairs. Assuming the car repair shop is engaged in actual fraud, once the fraud becomes known to consumers, alert entrepreneurs begin to recognize a profitable opportunity. In the presence of creative destruction, the fraudulent firm would get pushed out of the market, because consumers would choose to do business with the fraudulent firm's innovative competitors who operate in a nonfraudulent manner. We illustrate this point through the counterexample of Gazprom, which shows how fraudulent actors can proliferate in markets inhibited by a lack of creative destruction.

Gazprom is a Russian majority state-owned multinational energy corporation. It produces a large share of the entire world's supply of natural gas and is one of the largest public companies in the world. The company is also rife with fraud and controversy, earning it the name "Russia's Enron."[15]

In 2000, Gazprom was accused of asset stripping after transferring hundreds of millions of dollars in assets outside the company in exchange for signing lucrative deals for personal gain by the company's executives. Later, Gazprom officials were accused of setting up shell companies to hide profits from shareholders.[16] In 2004, Gazprom was embroiled in the Yukos Oil fraud, a $35 billion tax evasion case believed to have been brought against the Yukos Oil Company as punishment for its owner's political opposition to the government of Vladimir Putin, and evaded state regulation following the government takeover. In 2011, leaked U.S. diplomatic cables revealed that the company was riddled with corruption, with Russian officials siphoning off Gazprom profits for political payoffs. In 2015, European Union (EU) regulators formally charged Gazprom for overcharging customers in five EU member states and engaging in anti-competitive behavior.[17]

Despite these accusations and the company's own poor management practices, Gazprom has endured. Why? Because the Russian economy is not characterized by creative destruction, and firms supported by the state face few incentives to act their best. This is especially true for the oil and gas industry, where the Russian state is heavily involved. Gazprom is majority state owned and finances the Russian political elite, who will not allow the company to fail. No matter how many times Gazprom dodges taxes, finances corrupt officials, or overcharges customers, it is likely to power onward thanks to its successful rent-seeking behavior.

Focus on Competition from Innovation

The third insight into the nature of capitalism considering creative destruction is that it is competition from innovation—not the neat picture of price competition favored by instructors of introductory economics classes—that determines capitalism's success. An example helps illustrate this point. Consider two gas stations: Bob's Gas and Sarah's Gas, each occupying opposite corners on a busy street. To lure in more customers, the owner of Sarah's Gas lowers her price of a gallon of gas by two cents. Fearing that customers will now flock to her station instead of his, the owner of Bob's Gas responds, lowering his price by three cents. Since the two stations are selling an identical product, the main thing that distinguishes them is their price—they are engaged in price competition. Consumers certainly benefit from this kind of competition, as they are spending less money at the gas pump.

Yet although Bob and Sarah are certainly concerned about their rival's pricing strategy, what really keeps each owner up at night is the growing number of electric vehicles (EVs) on the road, and the new EV charger that was installed down the street. The survival of each corner gas station is determined not by whether the other station charges a cent or two less for gas, but rather by whether consumers will even want gas at all in the future! In that case, innovating will be the gas stations' only chance of survival. Were EVs to gain a growing share of the market, Sarah and Bob could both install EV chargers at their stations and compete against each other by providing the goods and services that customers are likely to demand while waiting for their cars to charge. Technological disruption threatens the survival of both gas stations equally. Schumpeter's insight was recognized by the economist and Nobel laureate George Stigler, who wrote: "Schumpeter painted an unconventional picture of the capitalistic process. The competition between the Pennsylvania and New York Central Railroads, he argued, might be sporadic and even trifling, but the competition to railroads provided by new transportation media such as trucks, automobiles, and airplanes really mattered. . . . We economists mostly rebelled against such heresy, but it left its mark."[18]

It is the competition between incumbent firms and innovators that animates Schumpeter's insights. This is also the kind of competition that truly matters once we realize that creative destruction is the essential driver of capitalism. The gains to consumer welfare necessary to produce the Great Enrichment came from technological leaps that rendered the status quo obsolete, not from incremental price cuts between firms with nearly indistinguishable product offerings. Why does this matter? The greatest threat many firms face is not from established competitors within their own industry but from smaller, nimbler upstarts offering novel technologies that threaten their market dominance. Today, Walmart's biggest competitor is not Target but Amazon. In the same way, the biggest competitors for American ice traders in the 19th century were not Russian or Norwegian producers but rather plant ice, which itself was replaced by modern refrigeration and cooling systems. History is replete with such examples.

Schumpeter's Vision

Capitalism's critics often judge it harshly because they fail to appreciate the centrality of creative destruction. Recognizing creative destruction as the essential driving force of capitalism forces us to adopt a vision for a dynamic world, one characterized by incessant change. We begin to see the world through Schumpeter's eyes. This vision focuses our judgment of capitalism on its long-term success in the form of higher economic growth. This vision changes how we view the economic and social structures of capitalist society, from, for example, how we view market power to income inequality to the presence of fraudulent behavior compared with other economic systems. Lastly, this vision for a dynamic world attunes us to the existential threats to the status quo from the creative destruction enabled by technological change.

We therefore should measure capitalism's success in any particular place—the United States, Germany, Japan—by the extent of creative destruction occurring within it. The extent of creative destruction in capitalist societies is how we know to what degree capitalism is working as it should. When creative destruction breaks down and stasis replaces dynamism, then the optimistic outlook of Schumpeter's vision wanes. When we observe something that slows or halts creative destruction—whether crony capitalism, welfare capitalism, or some other top-down economic system—we are not witnessing the capitalism of Schumpeter's vision.

4

Innovation Creates
Even as It Destroys

Innovation Drives Creative Destruction

The gale of creative destruction Schumpeter describes
blows into the sails of capitalism. If the essence of capitalism is change—changes in products, changes in jobs,
changes in firms—then creative destruction is the vehicle
through which most change comes about. Taken as a whole,
these changes have been for the better, as evidenced by the
Great Enrichment. If improvements in the quality of goods
and services are included—for example, the difference in
the quality of a cellphone in the 1980s versus a smartphone

today is not fully reflected in price changes—then real incomes have risen at least 3,000 percent since 1800.[1] Life expectancy has skyrocketed over that same period thanks to the great technological inventions affecting our everyday lives: electricity, the internal combustion engine, chemical engineering, communications, and plumbing. Thanks to creative destruction, the average person today lives a life that is longer, safer, and more affluent than those of our ancestors.

Innovation—the focus of this chapter—has largely fueled these gains. Innovation is central to the definition of the term "creative destruction" itself—the "creative" refers to the entry of new innovations into the market, while the "destruction" refers to the fate of the status quo when those innovations collide with the established way of doing things. This chapter will delve into both halves of the formula—the creation and destruction of Schumpeter's gale, outlining his theory as described in *The Theory of Economic Development* and *Capitalism, Socialism and Democracy*—and explore how the two concepts are interlinked. One cannot exist without the other. Without creation, there is no impetus for destruction; without destruction, there is no room for new innovations to flourish.

Schumpeter's Theories of Innovation

Let's start by unpacking the creative half of creative destruction. What is required for creation? Schumpeter's *Theory of Economic Development* offers three components: innovations, credit, and innovators.[2] When all three are properly combined, creative destruction is realized, and with it, the many benefits for society that help sustain the Great Enrichment.

The first component to the theory is innovations. An innovation is an invention that has been "carried out," Schumpeter's way of describing an invention that has been widely operationalized in the real world and what we would today characterize as "brought to market." Think of products that made the jump from the research laboratory to the drugstore shelf, or of a new warehouse layout that moves from a blueprint to the real world. A contemporary example of bringing an invention to market to create innovation is the Xerox Alto. The Alto, first developed in 1973 by PARC, Xerox's research division, was the first computer to feature a mouse and graphical user interface. At the time, Xerox executives had no idea how revolutionary a product they had. The Alto was a technology demonstrator, not intended for a consumer mass market—it was an invention, not an innovation. In 1979, Apple cofounder Steve Jobs saw a demonstration of the Alto and instantly saw the tremendous commercial applicability of the mouse and graphical user interface.[3] Apple engineers used the Alto as inspiration for the Apple Macintosh computer. The introduction of the Macintosh with the mouse and graphical user interface transformed the Alto's underlying technologies from inventions to innovations.

The tremendous increase in living standards that has characterized the Great Enrichment is powered by more than just a computer mouse. The scope of what an innovation can be extends far beyond physical products to new business models, new ways to harness resources, and new ways to produce. Schumpeter offers five different categories of innovations, all of which have the potential to provide the impulse for creative destruction.[4]

The first category is a new good or quality of good. This category best fits with the popular characterization of innovations as tangible products, either completely new ones (the iPhone) or improvements on existing ones (the iPhone 2). Notably, this definition also includes services (the first iPhone repair store). It is easy to see how this type of invention helped realize the Great Enrichment. Indoor plumbing and wastewater systems, for example, massively improved sanitation in urban environments, largely eliminating the disease-carrying sewage that would spew onto city streets.

The second category is a new method of production—think of a reorganization of a factory floor or a new method of synthesizing a lifesaving drug. New kinds of innovation, especially the introduction of mass production, also helped realize the Great Enrichment. In Chapter 2, we encountered Schumpeter's example of the capitalist achievement being the availability of silk stockings for not only queens but also factory girls. Creative destruction enables the replacement of antiquated methods of production with more efficient means, driving down costs and making goods and services more affordable.

The third category is the opening of new markets. A primary example is international trade. Goods sold in a home market and then introduced to a foreign market where they did not previously exist act like Schumpeter's first category of innovation, creating new goods and potentially displacing incumbent domestic offerings. Trade increases the variety of available goods for consumers, and the intensified competition can increase domestic productivity by forcing less productive domestic firms to exit the market.

The fourth category is the discovery of a new source of supply. Often, this kind of innovation is prompted by advances in Schumpeter's first two categories. The shale oil boom experienced by the United States in the 2010s offers one such example. The introduction of fracking—a process by which high-pressure liquid is injected into subterranean boreholes to force out oil and gas—is an example of a new method of production that led to the discovery of new sources of hydrocarbons in the U.S. Midwest.

The fifth category is what Schumpeter calls the carrying out of a new organization of an industry—what we would commonly understand today to be a merger or acquisition, for example. Mergers and acquisitions ostensibly help lead to efficiency and productivity gains, consolidating duplicated resources between the merged parties and allowing for greater economies of scale. Recent evidence on this question has been mixed,[5] but, at the very least, a reorganization punctures the status quo equilibrium, offering fuel for creative destruction.

From our Schumpeterian theoretical toolkit, we now have five diverse kinds of innovations that can jump-start the creative destruction process. Yet the innovation on its own is not enough for creative destruction to do its magic. To be brought to market, innovations require credit, the second component in the creative destruction process. Credit is necessary because innovations are brought to market using the people, equipment, ideas, and resources of their time—what economists would call "the existing means of production." Credit provides the financial firepower necessary to harness these means and realize an innovation's potential. Credit turns ideas into inventions and inventions into innovations by bringing them to market. Without credit, there is no innovation and no creative destruction. Thus, where and how credit is allocated have a big impact on economic growth. Credit allocated toward highly productive innovations is likely to create more growth, whereas credit squandered on less productive innovations will harm the economy's growth relative to where it could have been.

Credit allocation is so important that capitalists, the providers of such credit, rightly play an outsized role in the economy. When Schumpeter was writing, the primary source of credit was bankers, who loaned fixed sums of money at an agreed-upon interest rate and repayment schedule. Today, two other such sources of credit would be venture capitalists and angel investors—individuals and institutions that offer capital in exchange for an ownership stake in the innovation. Schumpeter placed great weight on the importance of credit to his theory, noting: "[The banker] is the capitalist par excellence. . . . He is the ephor of the exchange economy."[6] Schumpeter was right that credit allocation is the keystone of the capitalist economy.

The importance of the capitalist is evidenced further by the fact that credit allocation is extremely difficult. Capitalists have no crystal ball; they cannot discern which innovations will succeed and which will fail. A properly functioning financial system ensures that capitalists will face high costs for bankrolling failed innovations, giving them strong incentives to try their hardest to direct their capital toward innovations that offer the greatest expected return. Finding the greatest return means funding innovations that redeploy resources to the ends most valued by consumers. That reallocation fuels the growth-enhancing creative destruction process from which we all benefit. In this way, the capitalist system helps funnel credit to where it is needed most for creative destruction to work.

Innovators make up the third component for the creative destruction process. Innovators can be individuals (singular entrepreneurs), groups of individuals, or even entire organizations (an institutional research lab) responsible for conceiving new inventions and transforming inventions into innovations. Like capitalists, innovators are central to economic growth because they tie innovations and credit together, marshaling the necessary resources and upending the status quo to bring about creative destruction.

In our discussion of innovators, we break down this section into two elements. First, we will discuss the sole innovator, known as the entrepreneur—the subject of much of Schumpeter's early writing on innovation and creative destruction. Then we will discuss the subject of Schumpeter's later works, especially in *Capitalism, Socialism and Democracy*: status quo innovators who work as part of existing organizations. Each class of innovator is distinct, with unique characteristics and economic effects.

The first kind of innovator is the entrepreneur. Early in his academic career Schumpeter was infatuated with the entrepreneur, writing an account in *The Theory of Economic Development* of a lone, mythic figure whose efforts heroically drove economic progress. While Schumpeter's account certainly romanticizes the entrepreneurial class, he offers penetrating insight into the psychology of entrepreneurs and their appetite for risk taking. In Schumpeter's view, entrepreneurs have two defining characteristics: psychology and impermanence.

Psychology

To Schumpeter, only entrepreneurs possess the psychological characteristics necessary to step outside the rhythm and routine of daily life and strive for success in business. He writes in *The Theory of Economic Development* that entrepreneurs are unique in their ability to break out of the humdrum of responsibilities that characterize ordinary occupations and instead swim against three forces of inertia that hinder entrepreneurship:

- **Economic uncertainty.** Economic uncertainty refers to the risk inherent with any innovation. Just as capitalists are uncertain as to whether their investments will pay off, prospective entrepreneurs also lack perfect information about the viability of their innovations. Perhaps the innovation will flop with consumers, or it will be too complicated to realize. Innovation is risky, so entrepreneurs need to have a higher risk tolerance than most other people.

- **Subjective reluctance.** Subjective reluctance refers to a prospective entrepreneur's distaste for the often-unpredictable entrepreneurial lifestyle. For example, a prospective entrepreneur may not wish to leave a stable, salaried job that offers plenty of family time in exchange for the late hours and personal accountability that come with being one's own boss.

- **Resistance from outside forces.** Prospective entrepreneurs may be discouraged by their spouses, family, or friends from pursuing their idea. They may face opposition from incumbent firms, capital markets, or an unforgiving regulatory environment determined to preserve the status quo.[7]

Given these obstacles, how do entrepreneurs push through? Here, Schumpeter's psychological portrait of the entrepreneur shines in all its romanticized glory. He argues that what separates prospective entrepreneurs from actual ones are three qualities possessed by the latter—qualities so powerful that they can overcome the three inertial forces:

(1) **"Dreams of a private kingdom."** This is the phrase Schumpeter uses to describe the entrepreneur's desire to build a legacy. Entrepreneurs innovate not just for their own well-being but to build wealth that will last for generations, providing affluence and respectability for their families.

(2) **The "will to conquer."** This phrase describes the sheer force of will successful entrepreneurs apply to removing obstacles in their way, and the personal satisfaction they derive from seeing their innovation conquer the status quo and become successful. To Schumpeter, this is where the competitiveness of the entrepreneur shines through.

(3) **The "joy of creation."** Entrepreneurs get satisfaction not just from accumulating wealth or crushing the competition but also from the process of creation, of

designing and realizing their invention and then trans-forming it into an innovation.

Successful entrepreneurs possess all three of these charac-teristics to varying degrees, enabling them to power through the economic uncertainty, subjective reluctance, and resis-tance from the outside world that deters so many prospective entrepreneurs.[8]

Impermanence

The second defining characteristic of entrepreneurs that Schumpeter identifies is their impermanence. What do we mean by impermanence? Someone can be described as an entrepreneur while in the process of turning an invention into an innovation—that is, bringing an invention to mar-ket. But once the innovation becomes an established part of the status quo, the entrepreneur is no more, and becomes a manager. A manager who innovates again becomes an entrepreneur once more.

The entrepreneur/manager distinction matters, as entre-preneurs need a different set of skills than managers do. Entrepreneurs need boldness, courage, and a willingness to break norms. Managers, on the other hand, are responsible for creating and enforcing those norms. One is geared to disrupt the status quo; the other, to preserve it. As a result, managers have a different set of policy preferences and attitudes toward creative destruction than do entrepreneurs. One major barrier to promoting creative destruction is that, since the entrepreneurial class is temporary, those who support pro-entrepreneurship policies are a very limited constituency!

Now that we've laid out the crucial ingredients for creative destruction in Schumpeter's *Theory of Economic Development*, how do the various pieces of the theory fit together?

The story of Joy Mangano, serial entrepreneur and inventor of the Miracle Mop, brings Schumpeter's theory to life. As described in the 2015 biopic *Joy*, starring Jennifer Lawrence, Joy Mangano is the quintessential Schumpeterian entrepreneur.[9] At the start of the film, Joy is an obsessive tinkerer who comes up with a breakthrough new combination after cutting her hands from wringing glass out of a mop. In response, she invents a self-wringing mop with a dense, absorbent cotton head—the Miracle Mop. With her new combination in hand, Joy needs credit to bring it to market. However, as a single mother with four generations of dependents and a live-in ex-husband, Joy is financially strapped. So she pitches her product idea to her father's wealthy girlfriend, takes out a second mortgage on her home to secure the loan, and pledges to dedicate all she has to making the Miracle Mop succeed.

Throughout, Joy overcomes the obstacles to entrepreneurship to attain success in business. At every step, she faces economic uncertainty. Is her innovation already patented? How many units should she produce? How should she sell her product?

She also faces her own subjective reluctance. Halfway through the film, Joy comes close to collapsing from her early failures. In one particularly dramatic scene, she comes home to deactivated phone lines, sick children, a twice-mortgaged home, and a pile of bills without a single mop sold. More than anything else, Joy faces resistance from outside forces. Her supplier rips her off. Her half sister attempts to tank Joy's business in a jealous ploy for their father's attention. The male executives of QVC—the TV home-shopping channel where she hawks her wares—do not take her seriously because of her gender.

Joy perseveres through these obstacles thanks to the Schumpeterian motivations for entrepreneurship. She is the perfect example of the joy of creation, constantly tinkering and designing helpful inventions around her overcrowded family home. She is motivated by the will to conquer, committed to using all means necessary to outcompete her business rivals while negotiating with a creditor.

Finally, she dreams of a private kingdom, a dream that comes true in the closing scenes of the film as her Miracle Mop becomes a roaring success and she lives comfortably with her family.

Joy Mangano is the kind of innovator who tends to capture our imagination. Schumpeter, too—perhaps owing to his youth in the dazzling Vienna of the early 20th century—was infatuated with the entrepreneur. Accordingly, much of his early work concentrated on the individual entrepreneur as the sole driver of innovation. However, innovations can also come from other sources—namely, incumbent firms. Think of research into new strands of nylon conducted at DuPont labs or technology companies feverishly adding new features to their signature platforms.

Later in his career, Schumpeter recognized his early omission in *The Theory of Economic Development* and, accordingly, expanded this definition of who was an innovator to include status quo players in *Capitalism, Socialism and Democracy*. Schumpeter envisioned such innovators as big research labs, replete with talent and funding to create new innovations. Given the vast resources at their disposal, especially in comparison with the humble entrepreneur, we would expect such large innovators to be the engines of technological advancement. However, there is quantitative evidence suggesting how difficult it is for incumbents to introduce successful innovations.[10] Why is this?

Schumpeter's own writing on the psychology of the entrepreneur, our first characteristic of innovators, may offer an explanation. Essentially, incumbent innovators face the same obstacles that entrepreneurs do but are unable to draw on the same motivations that help propel entrepreneurs to succeed.

Economic uncertainty is always a given for new and untested innovations. Both also face resistance from outside forces. In the case of incumbent innovators, such resistance may take the form of the company leadership or shareholders dictating where resources should be allocated in the pursuit of different innovations or from uncooperative research team members.

They also face subjective reluctance, albeit of a different character. For entrepreneurs, Schumpeter argued that subjective reluctance can take shape as an individual's unwillingness to step out of the comfort of his or her daily routine and into the unpredictability of the entrepreneurial lifestyle. For established innovators, however, innovation is their daily routine!

By contrast, established companies cannot draw on many of the qualities that drive entrepreneurs to overcome other obstacles to innovation. Employees of existing firms are unlikely to personally reap many of the benefits of their innovation; with few exceptions they cannot establish dynastic companies from their work or derive personal satisfaction from outcompeting business rivals. As a result, institutional researchers may not have the same will to conquer or wake up with dreams of a private kingdom that motivate so many entrepreneurs. In addition, as Schumpeter notes, innovation carried out by large incumbent firms can be dreary, routine, and lacking in imagination, reducing the joy of creation. When undertaken in the context of a large corporate bureaucracy, innovators may feel like cogs in a machine, unable to move at the speed and scale they desire.

Although Schumpeter's framing of the entrepreneur's psyche is romanticized to a degree, status quo players attempting to innovate really can struggle. Many are dragged down by institutional inertia, which can reduce the speed of innovation or the ability to spot the commercial potential of an invention. Some do not even recognize the need to innovate at all, assuming that because they have been successful in the past, they will continue to be successful in the future. Creative destruction tends to punish this mentality, as the next chapter will examine by way of two case studies.

Schumpeter's theory offers a clear-cut line between two kinds of innovators: entrepreneurs and large incumbent firms. In practice, however, the line between the two is much blurrier. Elon Musk offers one such example. Bouncing between innovations, Musk creates as an entrepreneur and then sets up an incumbent firm to push forward research and development (R & D) on the idea in his wake before bouncing on to the next innovation. While working as an "entrepreneur" on his next innovation, Musk also wears the "manager" hat at the incumbent firms he helps direct. On any given day, Musk may be working as an entrepreneur on the Boring Company's HyperLoop while managing Tesla and SpaceX as their institutional R & D labs push out new electric cars and rockets.[11]

Supporting Innovation

Now that we have set up all the requisite ingredients for innovation, we turn to considering the critical question: Given how important innovation is, how can we enable it? One irony is that, if successful, innovators become the status quo. In the hands of ingenious innovators, an invention properly brought to market and backed by investors or credit will flourish, often displacing existing offerings.

As the ripple effects of creative destruction subside, the innovation becomes part of the status quo that it originally disrupted. The nature of creative destruction is such that fresh entrants and innovations are inevitable, so this new equilibrium will always be challenged! Thus, innovators who once bulldozed through the status quo will always need to defend their position against Schumpeter's gale. They generally have two options: (a) continue to innovate faster than the competition or (b) stifle potential challengers. Since it is often difficult for incumbents to innovate for the reasons discussed earlier, incumbents tend to direct their economic resources toward stifling the creativity of challengers. Incumbents lobby not for free markets but for protections: tax breaks, subsidies, and regulatory protections. All of these create barriers to entry and prevent creative destruction from occurring as it should. Thus, to best promote innovation, policymakers should lift such barriers to entry and deny firms that appeal for new ones.

Enabling innovation requires more than just designing good policies that support innovators, because innovation tends to leave a destructive swath in its wake, and such destruction engenders resistance. Schumpeter knew this; his theory was called not just "creationism" but creative destruction for a reason. Policies designed to support innovation must also acknowledge the resistance to innovation and offer ways to salve it. Failing to do so does a disservice to the displaced and can have negative and even violent consequences.

The Luddites offer one famous historical example. Active in Britain during the 19th century, the Luddites were a secret organization of textile workers who destroyed textile machinery in protest of the mechanization of their industry.[12] Thanks to the advent of the Industrial Revolution, the British textile industry was reorganizing itself around large factories instead of individual cottage workshops that had been the rule for much of English history. Because of their willingness to violate costly yet historically rooted methods of production through machinery, factory owners required far fewer workers to produce even more textiles than under the old method of organization. Many textile workers lost their jobs and resorted to violent protest, smashing stocking frames, cropping frames, and cotton-weaving looms in frustration at their economic misery. The Luddite movement became so widespread that the British Army was deployed to contain it. Luddite protestors had bloody clashes with British troops on several occasions—in 1808, the British had dedicated more soldiers to suppressing the Luddites than to fighting Napoleon on the Continent.[13]

We do not believe that the solution to dealing with the social consequences of innovation is to prevent innovation from ever destroying the status quo. As we discussed in Chapter 3, only by allowing destruction to take place can labor and capital be reallocated to help the economy enjoy the kind of sustainable, long-run economic growth that has helped sustain the Great Enrichment. Bailouts for ailing firms, single-source noncompetitively awarded government contracts, state payroll support for companies, preferential tax credits, and labor laws restricting workers' ability to freely change jobs are all examples of policies that do more harm than good because they stop innovation, which benefits all, to help the few who are directly affected by the destruction. Moreover, our focus is on the long-term objective of higher economic growth. To help those whose livelihoods are taken away by innovation, we think that better policy options exist than simply restricting innovation.

At this stage of our book's narrative, we have developed all of the essential economic points for understanding creative destruction. We know what Schumpeter's concept means, why it is important for economic growth, how it influences our view of capitalism, what causes it, who initiates it, and its tendency to generate resistance. Let us then turn next to two contemporary case studies that bring together all of these different economic elements of creative destruction.

5

The Fall of Blockbuster and the Rise of Uber Teach Us Different Lessons

Blockbuster and Netflix

The year is 1997. It's Friday night—movie night! You hop in the car to drive a few short minutes to the nearby Blockbuster. Opening the door, a blast of frigid air knocks back the hot summer evening, and you step into a bright blue-and-yellow world whose neon lights stand in stark contrast to the dreary strip mall outside. Rows of new movies flash out at you from the front shelves: *Independence Day*, *Space Jam*, and that Baz Luhrmann remake of *Romeo and Juliet* your wife keeps raving about.

As you wander the aisles looking for your Friday night escape, Blockbuster's bright, colorful sheen fades, replaced by the grimy signs of heavy foot traffic. There's a stain on the kids' aisle carpet, and the paint on the shelves is nicked and chipped. Having picked out your movie—Quentin Tarantino's *Reservoir Dogs*—you find the checkout line an exercise in patience. Kids duck and weave around their parents' legs. Customers gingerly step around a spilled bag of candy as a couple argues over who is responsible for forgetting to return *The Usual Suspects*.

Finally making your way to the front of the line, the teenager working the counter hits you with bad news: a $40 late fee for *Apollo 13*. You grumble and grouse, but it's movie night, and you have no other good rental options. As you cough up the cash to pay the late fee, you can't help but wonder if there's a better, more convenient way to rent movies, without late fees.

A version of this story is what Reed Hastings, Netflix cofounder and chief executive officer, would give at venture capital pitches and media appearances when explaining the genesis of the Netflix idea and the problem it aimed to solve.

Hastings now admits that he did not actually pay $40 to Blockbuster in late fees for *Apollo 13*.[1] Yet the true story of how Netflix came to be is much messier than a packaged media anecdote. Reality, as with even the purest cases of creative destruction, is often muddy, nonlinear, or, as Schumpeter would put it, *dynamic.*

This chapter digs into some of those dynamics, first discussing the competitive interplay between Netflix and Blockbuster as a "pure" example of the theory of creative destruction. It profiles a case in which the benefits of creation became widely accepted, even with the accompanying destruction. This case stands in contrast to the second part of the chapter, which will offer another case in which repeated attempts have been made to halt creative destruction.

To understand Netflix's founding story, we first must delve into how Blockbuster became so dominant in its time. Most prior analyses[2]—books, documentaries, and articles—have focused on Netflix's half of the story and the disruptive innovations it brought to bear: the delivery model, the elimination of late fees, the jump to streaming. From this perspective, Blockbuster's destruction seems inevitable. Yet hindsight is 20/20. For over two decades, Blockbuster was a colossus and household icon, with nearly 10,000 stores and 81,000 employees.[3] It was the first video rental service to serve billions of home videos to a mass audience and popularized the VCR. By 2019, however, only one Blockbuster in Bend, Oregon, remained—a stunning collapse.[4] How did this come to be?

Blockbuster was founded in 1985 by David Cook, an entrepreneur and business owner who provided computer software to the Texas oil and gas industry.[5] Using his experience in data management, Cook built a predictive shelf-stocking model for a new type of video rental store. Unlike other video stores at the time, which were typically independently owned and operated, Cook designed Blockbuster to work off a hub-and-spokes model, whereby a central warehouse holds huge stocks of new movie releases and uses Cook's predictive model to ship the right types and numbers of movies out to individual stores.[6] His warehouse-centric strategy was a huge success. Since inventory was concentrated offsite, it was cheap to open new Blockbuster stores, and the number of locations shot up. The more accessible Blockbuster became, the more people wanted to rent there, and the more stores the company opened. In just two short years, Blockbuster had already attracted the attention of Wayne Huizenga, an American serial entrepreneur and investor, who spotted the company's significant growth potential.[7]

In 1987, Huizenga acquired Blockbuster for an undisclosed sum and the company's growth went supersonic. From 1986 to 1992, Blockbuster grew from 3 to 2,800 stores and had opened overseas locations in the United Kingdom—at one point, Blockbuster was opening a new store every 17 hours![8] In 1992, the company owned 13 percent of the total U.S. market share for video rentals and was larger than its next 300 biggest competitors combined.[9]

Blockbuster was a media behemoth, and, as Schumpeter would predict, began to act with the confidence and complacency of one. In a 1992 earnings call, Vice-Chair Steven Berrard remarked to shareholders: "We believe it's just too tough for anybody to catch us. . . . No single company has the presence or recognition of Blockbuster."[10] Wall Street largely concurred. That same year, one analyst from Southeast Research Partners noted, "[Blockbuster's success] flies directly in the face of many critics that say technology is going to obsolete the video store."[11] Blockbuster's meteoric growth continued throughout the 1990s and into the 2000s—at the peak of the company's growth in 2004, it had 9,100 stores and employed 84,300 people.[12]

Blockbuster's rapid ascent is matched in scale only by the speed of its decline. In just 16 years, 9,099 of those stores had closed.[13] Blockbuster was standing in the way of a confluence of new technologies, business models, and competitors all gunning for the top spot in the multibillion-dollar world of video rental. Even worse for Blockbuster, from Schumpeter's theory of innovation, discussed in Chapter 4, we know that incumbent firms can be *hefty*, which makes them slow to innovate and vulnerable to being undercut by creative destruction. Thus, the blame for Blockbuster's demise falls not on the shoulders of its leadership alone—in a sense, the disruption was perhaps inevitable. Blockbuster's confidence made it vulnerable to the two primary threats circling the waters.

The first of those threats was DVD technology. At the time of the DVD's emergence in the mid-1990s, the VCR/VHS technology was king. VCR players were comparatively inexpensive, but the VHS tapes they played were not. Purchasing large numbers of tapes was out of reach for many households, hence the popularity of rental services like Blockbuster, which let customers borrow an expensive VHS tape for just a few bucks.[14] DVDs threatened to upend this business model. They were smaller, cheaper, more durable, did not have to be rewound after watching, and offered better picture quality than VHS tapes. Hollywood studios recognized that the higher quality and lower cost of the DVD would enable them to sell their movies directly to the public. This was a serious threat to a rental service like Blockbuster, which functioned as an intermediary between the expensive, studio-produced VHS tapes and budget-conscious consumers.

Blockbuster, however, was offered an early way out of this predicament. In 1997, Warner Brothers, one of the top Hollywood studios, offered Blockbuster a deal whereby Blockbuster could rent out Warner Brothers DVDs before they were sold directly to the public. In exchange, the studio would get a 40 percent cut of the sale.[15] A skeptical Blockbuster turned the deal down; Warner Brothers responded by substantially lowering its wholesale DVD prices and instead extending the same deal to Walmart, which accepted it. As a result, Walmart quickly surpassed Blockbuster as studios' biggest source of revenue.[16] Schumpeter would not be surprised. As Chapter 4 notes, incumbent firms often get wedded to the traditional way of doing things and tend to assume that prior successes guarantee future ones. The result is complacency and an unwillingness to change in response to a shifting business environment. Here Blockbuster is the rule rather than the exception.

The second of those threats was a new subscription-based business model that did away with late fees. Blockbuster infamously made a lot of money from late fees—in 2000, late fees were an $800 million revenue stream, a full 16 percent of Blockbuster's total revenue.[17] However, they also generated substantial consumer resentment. Late fees could double or triple the cost of a video rental, allowing Blockbuster to keep sticker prices for rentals low but often ambushing forgetful customers at the checkout stand. Not only did customers dislike Blockbuster's model; they now had alternatives. Compounding the company's woes was the emergence of competitors that offered subscription-based models in which consumers would pay a flat monthly fee for the right to check out a fixed number of movies for as long as they held the subscription. Customers fed up with Blockbuster's late fees were able to quit renting from Blockbuster in favor of these new entrants: Netflix (founded in 1997) and Amazon Video (founded in 2006). Redbox would also join the competition for customers in 2002 by offering rentals via vending machines.[18]

Blockbuster was aware of this problem but fumbled its response. In 2000, when the company's competitors were still in their infancy, Blockbuster had an opportunity to purchase a financially distressed Netflix for $50 million—a pittance against Blockbuster's enormous size.[19] In a now-ironic moment, Netflix cofounder Marc Randolph notes that Blockbuster CEO John Antioco and other executives laughed the Netflix leadership out of the room! Again, Schumpeter would not be surprised. Incumbents often suffer from hubris that distorts their ability to see the competitive picture and their vulnerabilities clearly. However, the blame is not entirely on Blockbuster. Some of it is due to the dynamics intrinsic to the creative destruction process. Incumbents have imperfect information. New innovations are always on the horizon; they can never be sure which will be successful enough when brought to market to threaten their commanding position. If Blockbuster had purchased every conceivable competitor, it would have had no money left to run its business!

Rather than buy up Netflix, in 2004 Blockbuster instead attempted to respond to its late fee problem by "eliminating" late fees—without really doing so.[20] The result was an unmitigated legal and public relations disaster and financial headache. The "elimination" of late fees was just a public relations stunt. In reality, a customer who did not return a checked-out item within a week after the due date would automatically be charged the retail price of the rental item minus the rental fee already paid using whatever payment method Blockbuster had on file for them. If customers returned the rental within 30 days, they were refunded the full retail price less a small restocking fee.[21]

With hindsight we can see that this was perhaps the worst possible choice for Blockbuster, for three reasons.

First, the company decided to forgo a significant revenue stream (albeit one that customers hated). A customer could hold on to a DVD rental for 30 days and be liable for only the small restocking fee, which about $1.25 in 2004 dollars.[22] Even if a customer failed to return the item within

30 days, a late-returned item could rack up far more in fees than Blockbuster would earn by requiring customers to purchase the rental outright. Indeed, the year before Blockbuster implemented the policy change, the company earned about $500 million in late fees, much of which evaporated.[23]

Second, because customers could hold on to DVDs for so long, Blockbuster began having issues with stocking new and popular releases, threatening its prized status as the Friday night movie destination.

Third, Blockbuster was not only losing revenue from late fees, but also angering the very customers it sought to lure back by the way the policy change was marketed. Lawsuits from Massachusetts and other states mounted, alleging that Blockbuster was not transparent about the new policy and was charging customers' credit cards without their permission. A California court ruled that Blockbuster's advertising was misleading.[24]

Amid all the headaches, Blockbuster ultimately reinstated the late fees after suffering significant reputational damage.

All of the preceding headwinds—DVD technology, the unsustainability of the late fees, and the emergence of new competitors—were compounded by another consequence of being a hefty incumbent: an enormous pile of debt. Blockbuster's rapid growth throughout the 1990s had led to its being acquired by media giant Viacom.[25] Since Blockbuster's business model generated significant positive cash flow, Viacom used Blockbuster to service a major leveraged buyout, saddling Blockbuster's balance sheet with billions of dollars in debt to finance the acquisition of Paramount, a major movie studio. With the rise of Netflix and the shift to online streaming services, Blockbuster's debt constraints ensured that the company would lack the resources to adequately respond even if it had been prescient enough to properly identify the coming storm.

If Blockbuster is the destruction half of creative destruction in our case study, Netflix is the creation. We tell Netflix's story through the lens of Schumpeter's *Theory of Economic Development*, as described in Chapter 4, with its three interrelated components: innovation, credit, and innovators. We begin with the innovators, a pair of entrepreneurs.

The Birth of Netflix

Netflix was founded by Marc Randolph and Reed Hastings on August 29, 1997, in Scotts Valley, California.[26] We have already noted that Schumpeter argued that successful entrepreneurs possess the ability to step outside the rhythms of the humdrum of daily life and strive for success in business. Hastings and Randolph fit that description—both were serial technology entrepreneurs. Hastings was a

Silicon Valley veteran who had successfully brought software startup Pure Atria to market. Randolph bounced from startup to startup before landing at Pure Atria as a marketing director.[27]

Both Randolph and Hastings were compelled by what Schumpeter called the joy of creating. Early accounts of Netflix's founding suggest it was birthed by four months of Randolph and Hastings's long carpool rides into work at Pure Atria along the traffic-snarled highways of Silicon Valley. On those morning drives, they would bounce around various business ideas, Randolph the idealistic dreamer making suggestions and Hastings the veteran shooting down unfeasible ideas. Randolph's memoirs suggest he was drawn to entrepreneurship from an early age, constantly tinkering in his family home and liking "headaches . . . a problem in front of me every day, something to chew on. Something to solve."[28]

Both men were also fueled by the Schumpeterian will to conquer. Randolph's memoirs state that he "found satisfaction in lining up all the tasks, investigating all the problems, and then working to solve them. I was in the basement, building something, knowing that someday in the near future I'd have to invite everyone else in to have a look."[29] Hastings made clear on those car rides that he sought nothing less than to totally upend how people consume entertainment, to make it cleaner and more convenient.

Finally, both men had the Schumpeterian dream of building an empire. Randolph's memoirs share a story from his early years about a conversation with his father, who encouraged him to "build his own estate" and never have to work for another person.[30] This formative advice fueled Randolph's entrepreneurial drive.

To succeed in bringing about an innovation, entrepreneurs first need an idea. For Randolph and Hastings, that idea was to create an online business that would capitalize on the rapid growth of the internet. On those early morning car rides into Silicon Valley, they churned through dozens of mail-order ideas inspired by Amazon's online book delivery service, from shampoo to dog food. They finally settled on a DVD mail-delivery service when Randolph mailed a DVD to Hastings's house and it came through intact.[31] Netflix was born.

Which Schumpeterian innovations did Netflix introduce in its days before the advent of the streaming revolution? Netflix was what Schumpeter would call the opening of a new market—no one had used the mail to deliver DVDs to households before. Within this Schumpeterian category were several innovations. First was the introduction of a subscription plan. In its early iteration, Netflix users would pay a flat monthly subscription fee for the right to hold up to four DVDs at a time, ordered from the Netflix website and mailed directly to the subscribers' homes. When subscribers were done with one DVD, they could simply mail it back in exchange for a new one. This business model not only had no late fees, but it could be used from the comfort of your couch—no more spilled candy and bickering in the Blockbuster aisles. Furthermore, this business model shifted a large share of the storage costs of DVD rentals from a Netflix warehouse to the consumer's home theater shelf.

The second innovation was a predictive algorithm on the Netflix website that would suggest new movies. After viewing each movie, users would have the opportunity to rate it, and the algorithm would use its users' watch history and ratings to predict what they might be interested in next. Such an innovation was crucial for Netflix's early success—the algorithm helped Netflix get by without the Blockbuster movie buff working the counter to make recommendations.

Netflix's final innovation was bulk DVD purchases of the latest and most popular film releases. This approach stood in contrast to Blockbuster's strategy of "managed dissatisfaction," whereby the company stocked only small numbers of the latest releases. When Blockbuster's only competition was other brick-and-mortar stores, "managed dissatisfaction" made some sense in that it kept costs down as less popular movies were less expensive, and it enabled Blockbuster to leverage the enormous backlog of old movies it had accumulated through its sheer scale.[32] With few hits in stock but a large back catalog, customers were likely to get their second or third movie choice—not bad enough to walk out without a movie, but not good enough to walk out fully satisfied either. Netflix instead chose to keep vast stocks of the latest releases on hand—enough to potentially deal with a surge in rental demand for them or to accommodate large numbers of subscribers holding on to new DVDs for extended periods.

Hastings and Randolph had the right background and temperament to turn a winning idea into a reality. All that was missing was the last piece of the theory of economic development: *credit*. As Schumpeter himself noted, "Talent in economic life 'rides to success on its debts.'"[33] Netflix would certainly agree. Randolph's memoirs describe how Netflix's earliest employees threw the initialism OPM around the office: other people's money![34] It turns out that other people's money also included a $2 million loan from Hastings, who was independently wealthy from his prior Silicon Valley pursuits. With credit, Netflix was able to build out a website and algorithm, create a library of 925 movie titles, and hire an advertising agency to raise awareness of Netflix's product on internet forums for movie junkies.[35]

Thanks to other people's money, Netflix was able to go from idea to reality. After just two years, Netflix was ready to scale and, in 1999, received a $30 million infusion from French venture capital firm Groupe Arnault to fund branding and marketing initiatives and to build out distribution channels.[36] Additional capital came in 2002, when Netflix launched its initial public stock offering, and the company's growth continued. In 2003, Netflix hit the 1 million subscriber mark.[37] By 2007, Netflix capitalized on yet another innovation—video streaming, launching the service the same year it delivered its 1 billionth DVD.[38] By 2010, powered in large part by the growth of its streaming business, Netflix achieved a market valuation of $8 billion.[39]

The growth of Netflix is the creation flip side of the destruction of Blockbuster's business model. With the right entrepreneurs, a good idea, and sufficient credit, innovation happens! Such innovation can be tremendously positive—most would agree that Netflix offered an improvement over the Blockbuster experience. In fact, Netflix's business model took Blockbuster's weaknesses and *exploited* them. Blockbuster's many store locations, once considered an asset, became too numerous for quality control and consistent management, leading many to become run down and to offer an inconsistent and unreliable user experience.

In contrast, Netflix was fully online, offered a user-friendly interface, and could be accessed from the customer's couch. Furthermore, Blockbuster's business model revolved around managed dissatisfaction—users could not always get their first choice of movie but could probably get their second. Netflix—first through bulk orders of the latest DVDs and later through an aggressive pivot to streaming—could more consistently offer subscribers their first movie choice. Finally, Blockbuster's revenue was fueled in large part by the infamously unpopular late fees. Netflix's subscription-based model sidestepped this issue entirely.

Faced with steep competition from Netflix, Blockbuster went into a nosedive. At Blockbuster's 2004 peak, the company had 9,100 stores, 84,300 employees, and $6 billion in revenue. By 2010, with Netflix's streaming service gaining momentum, Blockbuster rolled out a streaming service of its own. However, just as Schumpeter predicted, the weight of incumbency blocked Blockbuster's ability to do so effectively. As a large public company, Blockbuster was hamstrung by a public and expensive board disagreement between activist investor Carl Icahn and CEO John Antioco over executive compensation and the company's strategic direction.

With a heavy debt burden and huge operating costs from its thousands of brick-and-mortar stores, Blockbuster was unable to afford the streaming pivot. By January 2010, Blockbuster shares were down 91 percent from their peak, and the company was delisted from the New York Stock Exchange. In 2011, Blockbuster filed for bankruptcy.[40] By 2019, only a single Blockbuster, in Bend, Oregon, remained.

The case of Netflix and Blockbuster is what we call a "pure" example of creative destruction. A powerful incumbent, Blockbuster, is threatened by new innovations: DVDs, a subscription model for video rentals, and streaming. Embodying those technologies is Netflix, a small yet highly creative competitor. Weighed down by its own prior successes, Blockbuster misses an opportunity to purchase Netflix, bungles its response to Netflix's business model, and has too much debt, boardroom drama, and physical store overhead to make a concerted push into streaming. The result: creation destroys, and Blockbuster is no more.

Taxicabs and Uber

Yet what happens when creation is not fully accompanied by destruction? Such is the muddied result of our next case study: the competitive interplay between ridesharing firms and the traditional transportation industry, with a focus on Uber and taxicabs in New York City. We call this an "impure" example of creative destruction because, as this case study will explore, the creation of Uber did not cause the destruction of the New York taxicab industry.

Unlike Netflix's relatively linear founding story, Uber's journey into New York City is much rougher, running into entrenched special interests, monopolies, and government protection that inhibited the development of Uber's innovation. Uber's story is one of a bare-knuckles brawl replete with playground name-calling, millions of lobbying dollars, and clashing political egos. This section of the chapter will discuss the tensions that can arise from the destruction half of the creative destruction process and what kinds of competitive responses incumbents—in this case, the New York City taxicab industry—can take to protect against new competitors.

To understand the response of the taxi industry to Uber, we must first dig into the history of the New York taxi industry and how it came to be operated as a publicly sanctioned monopoly.

Taxicabs had an ill-fated first introduction to New York City. The first New York taxi company was Samuel's Electric Carriage and Wagon Company (ECWC), founded in July 1897 with 12 electric cab cars.[41] Taxicabs were a faster and cleaner way of getting around the streets of New York, which were often clogged with horse manure. By the early 1900s, the ECWC had a fleet of over 1,000 taxicabs running in the city. The ECWC was not to last, however. Between a fire and the Panic of 1907, the ECWC collapsed. Taxis did not appear on the streets of New York City again until late 1907. Recognizing the market potential for taxis, a new entrant—New York Taxicab Company—began providing taxi service in late 1907. Painted yellow to be visible from a distance, the taxi was now here to stay.

One irony of the competition between taxicabs and Uber is that the taxicabs themselves were once the innovators. Taxis arose out of the creative destruction of the horse-drawn carriage—the primary mode of transit in New York City at the time. Taxis released no horse manure, making city streets more pleasant and sanitary. They moved around much more quickly than horses and required no rest. As a result, by the 1930s, the New York taxicab industry had ballooned. New York was now home to over 30,000 taxicab drivers. With such stiff competition from other drivers, cabbies worked longer hours and charged ever-lower fares.[42] Combined with the economic woes of the Great Depression, many riders became concerned about safety, fearing that cab drivers were deferring the maintenance necessary to ensure the mechanical integrity of their taxis.

Out of these concerns came the first push to create a public monopoly for taxis. The idea was simple: the City of New York would hand out a fixed number of taxi licenses, called medallions. Supporters argued that medallions would artificially limit the supply of taxis, pushing up the price of taxi rides but reducing congestion on city streets and ensuring that New Yorkers would have safe rides. In 1937, Mayor Fiorello La Guardia signed the Haas Act, which introduced the official taxi license and medallion system still in use today.[43] Initially, 16,900 taxi licenses were issued—a number that fell to 11,787 as many Depression-strapped drivers could not afford the $10 annual renewal fee (equivalent to $215 in 2023) necessary to keep the license.[44] As the U.S. economy recovered after the Great Depression, so did the demand for taxi services. However, the city kept the number of licenses the same. With ballooning demand and stagnant supply, medallion prices skyrocketed.

Unsurprisingly, with the massive growth of the medallion's value came regulation. In 1974, the New York Taxi and Limousine Commission (TLC) was created. With jurisdiction over medallion-sanctioned taxicabs, the TLC was designed to enforce safety standards, oversee the sale of medallions, set taxi fares, and protect public safety. Unionization also followed the growth in medallion prices.

In 1998, a drivers' union—the New York Taxi Workers Alliance (TWA)—was founded; about one-third of all New York taxi drivers joined at its inception.[45] Years later, both the TLC and TWA became powerful, entrenched incumbents who sought to block Uber's growth.

Thanks to the medallion system, New York City taxicabs had become a publicly sanctioned monopoly. New entrants were blocked. Medallion prices rose to sky-high levels, and cab companies ran their market space uncontested by competitive forces. It is no surprise then that the New York taxi industry was blindsided by a novel approach to urban transportation that upended how the industry had operated since the days of the horse-drawn buggy. Perhaps no company represented this shift better than Uber, herald of the "gig economy," which significantly challenged how taxicabs everywhere do business today. Why was Uber so disruptive? As with our prior case study, we will start from the beginning of Uber's story.

Uber was founded in 2009 as UberCab. Similar to how Netflix was supposedly founded by Reed Hastings's frustration at a $40 late fee for *Apollo 13*, cofounders Travis Kalanick and Garrett Camp tell the story of how Uber was inspired by their inability to get a cab ride during a Paris snowstorm, resulting in their being stranded outside for the night in the freezing Parisian snow.[46] Like Netflix, Uber had all the right ingredients in the Schumpeterian secret sauce.

First, what was Uber's Schumpeterian innovation? Schumpeter would identify it as both a new product and a new way to organize an existing industry—in this case by creating an on-demand ride service, accessible through a smartphone app that links drivers with customers. Central to the Uber innovation is a labor reorganization. Unlike drivers for traditional taxi companies, Uber drivers are categorized as independent contractors, not employees. This means that Uber drivers provide their own vehicles, gas, and car maintenance—a significant cost advantage for Uber over taxicab companies. In exchange, drivers can freely choose their hours. With some exceptions, which we will discuss later this chapter, Uber drivers may drive for as many or as few hours as they wish. In this sense, Uber is merely a clearinghouse, linking drivers' idle time and capital equipment—their cars—with riders.

Second, UberCab enjoyed early and ready access to the second ingredient of Schumpeter's secret sauce: credit. The company was seeded by Napster cofounder Shawn Fanning in its early funding stage with $1.25 million.[47]

Third, the company had two serial entrepreneurs—Kalanick and Camp—who were able to marshal the concept and funding into a workable product.

In June 2010, UberCab launched as Uber in San Francisco.[48] Explosive growth soon followed. Uber's growth was directly powered by its product's growing popularity, which created a positive feedback loop. As more and more people heard of Uber and downloaded its app, the pool of available Uber riders grew, creating greater demand for Uber drivers. With more drivers, Uber rides became ever easier to book, encouraging even more people to sign up for the app. By 2013, the company was earning more than $100 million, and by 2019 its revenue had leaped to $13 billion.[49] Much of this growth came at the expense of traditional taxicab companies, as the next section of the case study will show.

Uber's sudden and explosive growth brought creative destruction to the transportation industry. For consumers, Uber's offering was clearly better than taxi services: cashless, available on demand, and often cheaper. The incumbent taxicab companies that managed to weather the Uber shock were forced to up their game—adopting Uber-like innovations like cashless payment machines in cabs, web-booking services, and lower fares—to keep up.[50]

However, creative destruction is not always guaranteed, especially when incumbents threatened by the destruction are powerful and entrenched, and have access to multiple levers they can pull to block the competitive advantage of new entrants. This has been true for Uber, as the service has been banned in places ranging from Taiwan to London. Here we focus on New York City as one such example of how the creative destruction process can be stopped, if only partially, through measures falling short of a total ban.

In 2011, Uber entered New York City. That year was a good one to be a taxi medallion owner. Two medallions had been auctioned off in October for $1 million each—the highest sale price ever seen at the time.[51] The value of taxi medallions was up 1,900 percent from 1981 to the 2011 auction date, making the medallion a better investment than the Dow Jones Industrial Average (up 1,100 percent over that same period). Medallion prices were kept artificially high thanks to restrictions in supply in the market for taxis.

As New York City grew in population and the economy recovered from the 2008 financial crisis, demand for taxi services continued to climb while the number of taxi medallions stubbornly stayed at its 1937 level. Medallion holders knew this and jealously guarded their value, defeating any proposal that might have increased the supply of taxis in the city. Taxi medallion holders shot down proposals to grow the number of taxis by issuing new medallions, as well as to permit livery cabs to pick up street hails outside the busiest streets of Manhattan.

Confident in their unassailable monopoly position and enjoying record returns, complacency reigned among the established taxi companies. After the record 2011 auction, TLC chair David Yassky told the *New York Times*, "It's a lot of money, and it is an investment that someone would not make without being confident in the industry and the future of the city." Colgate University professor and taxi industry historian Graham Hodges affirmed the sentiment, telling the *Times*: "No one is very good at forecasting the economic future right now, but I would say [the taxi medallion is not in a bubble]. . . . It will always make good money and pay for itself. . . . There are certain things that are just gilt-edged assets, and this is one of them."[52]

Kalanick and Camp must not have read that day's edition of the *Times*. Uber's innovative business model was completely alien to the comfortable, government-granted monopoly. Uber was, technically, not a taxi company—its drivers were independent contractors—so it did not require medallions to operate on the streets of New York City. The result was that from 2011 to 2015 the number of for-hire vehicles in New York ballooned by 60 percent, to 63,000 total, of which 20,000 were Uber vehicles.[53] Still more belonged to other rideshare companies imitating Uber's technology and business model. This substantial increase in the supply of available for-hire vehicles was a significant negative shock to the hapless taxi companies, which couldn't do anything more than brandish their fists at the new drivers filling New York's streets.

As an indicator of the pent-up demand for additional taxi services, the number of completed Uber trips soared from 300,000 in 2013 to 3.5 million in 2015. Much of Uber's spectacular trip growth came at taxis' expense. An analysis of Uber and taxi commission data by *The Economist* in 2015 suggests that about 65 percent of Uber rides in that 2013–2015 period replaced taxi rides.[54] Notably, taxi rides saw their sharpest decline late at night when Uber was most active, falling 22 percent between the hours of 11:00 p.m. and 5:00 a.m., whereas trips at all other times of day fell by only 12 percent. Unsurprisingly, by 2015, just four years after Uber began operating in New York, the average auction price of a taxi medallion had fallen to $690,000.[55]

Taxi drivers and medallion holders alike suffered; however, New York residents benefited substantially. The average Uber trip was less expensive than a taxi trip. Uber cars were often cleaner and could be easily hailed with the tap of a smartphone screen. Before Uber, taxicab companies reigned supreme over New York City and could be choosy about where to pick up riders. This meant that cabs would heavily concentrate their services on the busy island of Manhattan, at the detriment of transportation accessibility for other parts of the city. This changed when rideshare services such as Uber entered the picture. As a competitive response to Uber, taxi drivers broadened their pickup areas to help make up for lost rides in Manhattan, making transportation more accessible to New Yorkers who normally saw little taxi service.[56]

The taxi industry—as the incumbents directly threatened by creative destruction—could not benefit much from these changes. But what recourse did they have? The medallion system clearly did not apply to Uber. Could other cumbersome regulations be imposed? Through the TWA, the taxi industry began lobbying New York City Hall—which gave them their monopoly protections in the first place—to eliminate, or at least blunt, the substantial competitive threat Uber represented.

The TWA had many levers it could pull to make that happen. The yellow taxi is one of the most iconic parts of New York City and is interwoven into its cultural fabric. With a reputation for boisterousness and a long history of political action, including strikes, the TWA was a well-entrenched constituency with a lot of weight to throw around. And it certainly brought that weight to bear on Uber. The drivers' union first used its close ties to Mayor Bill de Blasio's office to get City Hall to lean on Uber. Accordingly, in 2015, the mayor's office fired the first shot, decrying Uber as "Wal-Mart on wheels" and a "job-killer." Mayor de Blasio personally attacked the California-based startup, comparing its negative social effects with those of large oil companies.[57] City Hall followed the mayor's strong language with legislation. In 2015, de Blasio's office proposed legislation limiting the growth of for-hire vehicle companies to just 1 percent per year—a medallion-like growth cap. If passed, this would have been a substantial blow to Uber, which was growing at 3 percent annually at that time. City Hall justified the proposal by arguing that Uber's blockbuster growth was responsible for slower Manhattan traffic speeds, and therefore the cap would benefit all New Yorkers by helping relieve congestion.

Uber did not take the regulatory proposal sitting down. New York City was a major growth market for the company, and, with Uber still a relatively young and unestablished company, a defeat in New York might inspire other U.S. cities to enact similar measures. The company fought back hard, hiring lobbyists and arguing that the de Blasio administration was "in the pockets of millionaires" who owned the taxi fleets and the medallions that Uber's growth was devaluing. After an extended lobbying battle, on July 22, 2015, the de Blasio administration dropped the 1 percent annual growth cap proposal thanks to sustained opposition as shown by criticism from the editors of the *New York Times*, *New York Post*, and *New York Daily News*, as well as a 2015 poll by the Ferenstein Wire that revealed that 66 percent of New Yorkers opposed the Uber annual growth cap.[58]

The TWA was not yet done trying to tame Uber, however. In 2018, City Hall tried again, proposing both a one-year cap on for-hire vehicle licenses and minimum driver pay rules.[59] Both proposals were a threat to Uber. The first would completely stop the company's growth in New York City, while the second would raise driver costs, undercutting one of Uber's primary competitive advantages over traditional taxicab companies. Uber pulled out all the stops to prevent the proposals from passing. Joining forces with its rideshare competitor Lyft, Uber pumped over $1 million into a public persuasion campaign to argue that the city legislation would make Uber more expensive and less accessible.[60] Uber also made the fight personal, introducing a new feature to its app called "de Blasio view," where riders would be shown what fare costs and wait times would look like if Mayor de Blasio and the City Council passed the proposed changes (they were worse).[61] The company also made targeted appeals, arguing that the continued growth of the service was necessary to support rides in predominately black neighborhoods outside Manhattan that taxis traditionally avoided.[62]

This time, however, the de Blasio administration was better prepared for a tussle with Uber and argued that regulation was necessary for two reasons.[63] The first was that Uber was reducing quality of life for all New Yorkers. The city presented data collected since the 2015 spat showing how Uber and other rideshare companies had flooded New York City's streets with additional vehicles, hampering traffic flow. The second was that Uber harmed both taxi and Uber drivers alike. The TWA lent significant support to this point, leveraging its clout to publicly back the city proposal. The drivers' union argued that the rise of Uber had created a destructive race to the bottom for over 100,000 Uber and taxi drivers. According to the TWA, since the supply of vehicles had grown so much, both Uber and taxicabs had been forced to reduce fares, pushing drivers into longer hours for less pay.[64] Eagle-eyed readers will notice here that the TWA was deploying an argument almost identical to the one that led to the creation of the taxi medallion system back in 1937.

City Hall had also cleverly timed the regulatory proposal. Since the last regulatory push in 2015, Uber's reputation had taken a significant hit in the public eye.[65] The company was marred by scandals ranging from sexual harassment allegations leveled against Kalanick and Camp[66] to the discovery of anti-competitive practices against rideshare rival Lyft.[67] In the chaos of the administrative shuffle, New York City's regulatory strike succeeded.

In August 2018, New York City passed the two regulatory proposals: the one-year cap on rideshare vehicle growth and the establishment of a permanent pay floor for drivers.[68] By February 2019, the pay floor was in effect and required that Uber drivers must earn at least $17.22 per hour after expenses.

Of course, the regulations New York City put into place had unintended consequences that harmed the very drivers they were meant to help. On April 1, 2019, Uber announced an indefinite suspension of new driver hires.[69] In an interview with *Politico*, transportation industry expert Bruce Schaller, former New York deputy commissioner for traffic and planning, attributed Uber's decision to the new city regulations on rideshare companies, especially the one-year moratorium on new for-hire vehicles.[70] Riders suffered too; Uber also declared that customers would face reduced availability and higher prices for rides.

The wage floor and city limitations on the number of Uber vehicles that could be active at any given moment prompted Uber to implement a new "lockout" system that harmed drivers even further. Under this system, drivers in New York could only log into the Uber app and earn money when given permission by the company's software, which restricted who could drive and when and gave preference to drivers who were logged on the most. Predictably, this was a horrible outcome for drivers. Many relied on Uber as their sole source of income, so to get driving time and earn money, some drivers resorted to sleeping in their cars with the Uber app active, just waiting for the moment that the app would allow them to log in and accumulate hours to be able to continue to drive in the future.[71]

The competitive interplay between Uber and the New York taxicab industry is an example of the race between innovation and competitive response. Permitting creative destruction can be valuable not only for the benefits of the innovation itself but also in the creative ways incumbents respond. In this case study, the rise of Uber forced taxicab companies to innovate by modernizing their taxi fleets with digital technology and expanding their service areas. These benefits can only be gained if innovation is allowed to persist despite the destruction wreaked on the status quo. In the case of Uber in New York City, innovation was stifled by the incumbent taxi industry, which lobbied for government protection when a competitive response proved insufficient to claw back lost ground. The result of these cumbersome regulations has been more harm than good; Uber drivers, taxi drivers, and New York City residents alike have all suffered. To benefit from creative destruction, we must first trust in its ability to work its growth-producing magic unhindered by City Hall bureaucrats.

The cases of Netflix versus Blockbuster and Uber versus the New York taxicab industry show both the power and limitations of creative destruction. Left to thrive in a free and functioning market, Schumpeter's perennial gale blows with incredible power—improving quality of life through innovation but sometimes leaving a trail of destruction in its wake, as in Blockbuster's case. However, the gale of creative destruction can be blunted or blocked entirely. When facing an entrenched industry capable of leveraging lobbying power to regulate innovation, creative destruction can be slowed, as in the case of Uber's clash with New York City's taxicab industry.

We recognize the collateral damage creative destruction can cause, but the cost of slowing down creative destruction in the form of lower economic growth is also large. Like Schumpeter before us, we must expand our field of vision to consider not only the economic but also the cultural, social, and political consequences of creative destruction. As the astute reader will guess, the consequences of the cases we have discussed in this chapter go far beyond the narrowly economic. This is true of creative destruction in general.

6

The Cultural, Social, and Political Consequences Are as Profound as the Economic

Two Mechanisms of Creative Destruction's Cultural, Social, and Political Consequences

Modern economists naturally tend to focus on the economic consequences of creative destruction, as they are more attuned to these types of consequences, given their field of professional expertise. We have done the same in Chapter 5. Introduce a new set of innovations embodied in the firm Netflix, and economists will rightly point out the first-order effects on the economy. If Blockbuster does not innovate, Netflix will take over the market for movie rentals, driving Blockbuster out of business and leaving its workers temporarily unemployed. Yet Netflix can expand to meet the demand for movie rentals and hire workers to do so. Through its innovations, Netflix transforms the economy's technological landscape, thus propelling economic growth forward and increasing standards of living.

Although creative destruction always has an economic impact, it can also have profound cultural, social, and political consequences. Schumpeter understood this point. He conceptualized creative destruction to describe the incessant transformations of the economy from within, but he knew those transformations could also transform the entire society in which we live. We have seen this wider set of consequences in examples throughout this book, such as how innovations in music delivery have changed not only the technologies we use to listen to music, but also our listening experience—as in the transition from mixtapes to playlists, for example.

The purpose of this chapter is not to rehash these previous examples but to highlight the importance of the cultural, social, and political consequences of creative destruction.

They are worth emphasizing for two reasons. First, as we have said, economists tend not to highlight these consequences. By filling in that information gap, we will paint a more complete picture for the reader of the consequences of creative destruction. Second, the noneconomic consequences of creative destruction can sometimes be far more important and disruptive than the narrow economic consequences, shaking the very foundations of society as a result.

The noneconomic consequences of creative destruction that we are considering typically occur via two mechanisms: (a) the sociopolitical effects of economic change and (b) the direct cultural effects of the innovations themselves.

A good example of the sociopolitical effects of economic change is the loss of jobs, which can lead to a host of additional sociopolitical changes. Consider a small town that loses its primary employer, a factory. Perhaps the employer's products are simply not in demand anymore because of technological innovation, changing consumer tastes, or other factors. The factory closes its doors, and half of the town is laid off as a result. Employment prospects are bleak. Neighbors try to help one another, but despair descends on the population as people struggle to make ends meet. Alcohol and drugs become a solace for some, as the bonds that hold families and the community together begin to fray. Despite the town council's best efforts to lure another employer to open a new factory, it becomes increasingly clear that it will be a long time before the next large employer comes to town.

In the meantime, the town's tax base has dwindled, and the cost of lobbying state officials and advertising the community's strengths to private employers is taking a toll on the town's finances. Cuts to public services have to be made. Children growing up after the factory closed its doors see the closure's personal toll on their parents' well-worn faces. The town begins to hollow out as the young move away to seek better prospects and the old are left behind to fend for themselves. Moving to a bigger city, these young urban migrants seek out employment, compete for jobs with local workers, and accept lower wages to establish themselves in the city and gain some stability in their lives. The city's natives bemoan the influx of migrants and resent the competition. Pushed out of their jobs, the natives organize and lobby the city government to do something about their unwanted new neighbors. City politics take an ugly turn. . . .

Creative destruction can contain the seeds for these types of sociopolitical changes. How often and to what extent these changes occur depend on the particular innovation and the size, intensity, and importance of the economic changes the innovation unleashes, all of which are not necessarily easily discernible beforehand.

In the case of Netflix, the story of our small fictitious town does not ring true. Netflix caused a period of distress for the individuals who lost their jobs when the local Blockbuster closed its doors, but that job loss was not concentrated in a single town. Instead, it was spread throughout the entire U.S. economy, making up only a small share of most local labor markets. The total job loss from Blockbuster due to Netflix was easily matched by (a) the job growth due to Netflix's own hiring and (b) broader labor-market adjustments in locales where Netflix was not hiring. This is why we rarely hear about the destruction Netflix unleashed in the labor market. Blockbuster's former employees moved on to other jobs, either previously vacant or newly created. But that does not mean Netflix did not usher in profound cultural changes.

In fact, Netflix is a good example of the second mechanism driving noneconomic consequences of creative destruction— namely, the direct cultural effects of the innovations them- selves. As Netflix's market share of the movie rental business grew and then exploded to replace Blockbuster as the mar- ket leader, it became clear that Netflix's mail-delivery ser- vice of DVDs would soon wipe away a fixture of cultural life in America—the Friday night trip to the local Blockbuster. Instead, movie watchers walked out to the mailbox to collect the next arriving movie rental. The rituals of American life had been altered. As more and more people switched to renting movies from Netflix, local Blockbuster stores closed. These closures were frequently described as the loss of a community center where people would cross paths engaged in a shared ritual.

What people lost in their local Blockbuster was replaced by the convenience of having movies delivered directly to their doors without the threat of late fees. This benefit of convenience highlights another cultural effect of Netflix's innovation: the time saved from not having to pack the kids in the family van and drive off to Blockbuster. Searching for movies also changed. Whereas previously consumers would browse the aisles of Blockbuster, take suggestions from the local movie buffs employed at the store, and choose from the available inventory, now they can scan through Netflix's entire catalog online. With so many choices available, consumers can choose search criteria to refine their browsing. Netflix's algorithm uses your rental history to suggest movies you might enjoy, which makes searching even easier. The downside of this approach is that the mix of movies being watched has possibly narrowed, or simply changed from the selection generated by the Blockbuster browsing method, with unknown cultural consequences. Moreover, Netflix's algorithm introduced the problem of information silos. It was so convenient to rent movies based on the watch suggestions that viewers ran the risk of always watching movies closely related to their previous preferences instead of branching out and sampling new types of movies across the cultural spectrum.

Then again, Netflix's algorithm likely served audiences with niche preferences even better, as those viewers could watch more movies of their preferred genre that were unlikely to be stocked in large quantities at their local Blockbuster. We cannot know for certain whether Netflix's algorithm led to cultural impoverishment with respect to cinema knowledge. What we do know is that Netflix's way of searching for rentals was dramatically different from browsing in the local Blockbuster.

Moving beyond the early years of Netflix and the initial innovations that catapulted the company to the position of market leader, it is now clear with hindsight that the largest cultural effect from the creative destruction ushered in by Netflix is the dawning of the age of streaming. Netflix showed the entertainment industry that the direct-to-consumer delivery model for movies was not only possible but also highly lucrative.

As Netflix moved away from delivering DVDs through the mail to streaming movies directly to a viewer's smart TV, computer, or other device, competitors took notice. Amazon Prime Video entered the market. Established media companies and TV and movie studios responded by creating their own streaming services, like Disney+ and Hulu. The year 2020 convinced many consumers that streaming technology was not only a source of entertainment but a vital connection to the wider culture, as people around the world hunkered down during the outbreak of the COVID-19 pandemic and looked to streaming for a moment of escape.

At the time of this writing, streaming remains a source of dynamism in the entertainment industry, whether it be podcasts, music, or video content. Some of streaming's cultural consequences are already evident. The first-order effect is, of course, the sheer amount of content consumed. The low cost of storage allowed by hosting content on servers has also enabled streaming services to better cater to niche tastes. Whether it be listening to recordings of indigenous music with rare musical instruments or watching YouTube videos on how to perfect your Lego building technique, users can craft their consumption along narrowly defined lines. These niche consumers can also find one another, as the commenting sections of streaming services clearly attest. In this way, streaming services can help build ties between people with common interests who otherwise would never meet. For example, commenters on and creators of Lego YouTube videos can exchange building ideas and even meet up at local Lego conventions.

The ease of accessing streaming content has forced analog competitors to respond by differentiating their products in ways that make consumption in the analog world more tactile and experiential. Movie theaters, for example, have responded to competition from streaming by investing in better amenities, like reclining chairs and higher-quality concessions. Although streaming is clearly a main source of entertainment consumption, for many consumers streaming highlights the loss of these types of in-person experiences in shared public spaces. These consumers long to browse for books and music in brick-and-mortar book and record stores. This yearning fuels both the supply and demand for these types of stores, an irony of the age of streaming being that independent book and record stores appear to be thriving.

Ultimately, the future of the entertainment industry is highly speculative at this point. Again, what is not speculative is that immense cultural changes have taken place since the days of the local Blockbuster.

Although the example of Netflix cleanly illustrates the consequences of creative destruction beyond the narrowly economic, we need to expand our field of vision to fully appreciate the power of creative destruction in the cultural, social, and political realms. Let us then consider two innovations that transformed how we communicate with one another—the introduction of the printing press to Europe by Johannes Gutenberg in the 15th century and the internet and social media in our own time.

The Printing Press

Much of Johannes Gutenberg's life remains shrouded in mystery. We know he was born circa 1400 in Mainz, a city nestled next to the Rhine River in Germany. Gutenberg was born into a well-off family, and his father worked at the local mint. Gutenberg the son was likely exposed to goldsmithing and metalwork through his father, which would have equipped young Gutenberg with the skills necessary to create his breakthrough innovation. It appears likely that he began to bring his printing press into reality during the late 1430s or early 1440s.[1]

The key innovation was the development of moveable metal type. The printing technology in use long before Gutenberg was born required printers to carve out each page of text on wood blocks. Gutenberg changed all that. His durable metal letters could be arranged to create one page of text and then reused and rearranged to create the next. By the 1450s, Gutenberg's method was refined enough to begin printing what became known as the Gutenberg Bibles. Although the Chinese invention of printing predates Gutenberg's innovation, Gutenberg was still the first to introduce the printing press to Europe. Moreover, the Gutenberg press spread rapidly and quickly ushered in "a decisive point of no return in human history."[2]

Gutenberg's innovation drastically reduced the cost of creating copies of the written word in the form of books. Before Gutenberg's printing press, the work of copying long documents was done by scribes toiling tediously for long hours to reproduce single copies, one at a time. The books emerging from Europe's scriptoriums were beautiful and highly durable, but their high cost kept them out of the reach of all but the wealthiest buyers. The money required to purchase such handwritten books meant that the knowledge embodied in books—and its dissemination—were controlled by wealthy clients, such as the Catholic Church in Rome.

Control over the written word—most frequently the word of God and its interpretation—meant the church wielded immense power over what information and theology were shared with and taught to the wider populace. As the owner of books, the Catholic Church could spread the message of God as revealed in the Bible and gain followers and converts to its cause, increasing the wealth and power of the church as a result. Gutenberg's printing press, and the many other competitors that emerged as the technology spread through Europe, thus posed a threat to institutions like the Catholic Church, which used its ownership over costly knowledge embodied in books to wield power.

The point is not that Gutenberg's printing press suddenly meant that printing books was cheap in an absolute sense— just try to print your own book, let alone reproduce the beautiful Gutenberg Bibles. Printing books on Gutenberg's press required substantial capital outlays for equipment, space to house the workshop, and highly skilled labor. The equipment needed to be created through innovation, which required solving many technical problems—including the arrangement of production, construction of the actual press, the engraving of the metal type, and the mixing of ink for use in the press. All these technical aspects meant that the press required skilled workers able to read and set the type accurately, an exacting level of detail beyond the reach of many workers. No, Gutenberg's printing press was not cheap. But once the technical problems were solved, workers were trained and skilled enough to operate the press, and books began to flow from the press, Gutenberg's method of printing books was *cheaper* than copying them by hand.

The direct economic effect of Gutenberg's printing press was a collapse in the cost of printing books from the heights of the scriptorium. What began as a single workshop in Mainz quickly expanded into a new industry throughout Europe. Barcelona, Modena, and Rome all had printing presses by 1475. Twenty percent of Danish, Dutch, German, and Swiss cities had printing presses by 1500. England, a relatively late adopter, had 15 printing establishments by 1545.[3] The expansion of the printing press and the resulting drop in the costs of printing books would eventually lead to the shuttering of Europe's scriptoriums, as scribes were no longer needed to copy books by hand.

This instance of creative destruction was the beginning of what came to be known as Gutenberg's Revolution, whose full cultural, social, and political effects still reverberate into our own time. The flood of books, and the information and knowledge they contained, washed over all of European society, destroying and remaking the contours of a world that had persisted for centuries. Cheaper access to books increased the value of becoming literate, and increased literacy fueled the demand for more books. The printing press would thus pave the way for the Enlightenment and the Scientific Revolution. It also enabled religious dissenters such as Martin Luther to challenge papal authority in the Catholic Church in what became the Protestant Reformation.

By the time Martin Luther published his *Ninety-Five Theses* in 1517, the printing press was in widespread use throughout Europe. The dissemination of Luther's ideas in Germany was accomplished with ease, as any local printer could simply rearrange his metal type and begin printing multiple copies at low cost. As Luther's ideas spread and engaged the minds of reform-minded clergy, further broadsides against the Catholic Church rolled off the printing presses, spreading the ideas of the Reformation throughout Germany and beyond. Exposure to local Protestant writings led to the passage of municipal Reformation laws in German cities, which were aimed at reforming religious services and the role of religion in public life.[4]

As in the case of taxicab drivers' resistance to Uber, the pope and the Catholic Church did not sit idly by when faced with the whittling away of Catholicism's unquestioned dominance. Rome used censorship and repression to try to reestablish papal authority, but open revolt soon broke out in Germany and northwestern Europe, eventually leading to the Thirty Years' War. Much blood was shed during the Reformation, a world-shaking act of creative destruction—and it was unleashed by the printing press. The result was the emergence of Protestantism as a competitor to Catholicism after centuries of Catholicism's unquestioned dominance.

The waves of creative destruction unleashed by the printing press did not stop with the innovation itself but continued throughout history. The printing press served as a mechanism to disseminate new and different ideas, which themselves contained the potential for further creative destruction. The cultural, social, and political effects of the printing press demonstrate not only the power of creative destruction to transform society, but also the way conflict over these effects threatens to undermine creative destruction. The more creative destruction threatens the status quo, the stronger resistance to creative destruction emerges. The Catholic Church attempted to arrest the spread of the ideas of the Reformation and was willing to shed blood to do so. Even now, new ideas are potential sources of creative destruction, which is why books are still so frequently censored, banned, and burned. The world continues to struggle with the waves of creative destruction unleashed by Gutenberg's Revolution.

The Internet

Today, the internet and social media evoke comparisons to the printing press. Both innovations drastically reduced the cost of reproducing the written word. Both have enabled successive waves of creative destruction. They are different in that the internet and social media spread information even faster and go beyond the written word to include video and sound. Coupled with the appropriate technology, they can provide each of us with our own personal digital printing press in our pocket in the form of a smartphone.

With regard to our focus on the cultural, social, and political consequences of creative destruction, there is another key difference between the printing press and the internet and social media. Gutenberg's printing press was introduced during the 15th century, so the benefit of time makes it much easier to trace its effects on developments as monumental as the Reformation, the Enlightenment, and the Scientific Revolution. By comparison, the internet and social media are still in their infancy, which makes pinning down their consequences with a high degree of confidence difficult. This is particularly true of social media and its perceived political consequences up to the present day, as the growth of social media platforms (Facebook was founded in 2004 and Twitter, now called X, in 2006) has coincided with major political disruptions, such as the Great Recession (2007–2009) and the COVID-19 pandemic (2019–2022).

Nonetheless, the internet and social media are transformative innovations with broad cultural, social, and political consequences. Moreover, these innovations *feel* big and world shaping, as they have seeped into so many aspects of life, especially since smartphones have made the internet so easily accessible from anywhere.

We are speaking in broad terms when we write about the internet and social media. The internet and social media consist of many different innovations, the consequences of which can vary significantly depending on which innovation is under consideration. A more nuanced discussion of the internet and social media is beyond the scope of this book, so we will collectively refer to the "internet" as the innovation that unleashed the creative destruction we are describing. Shelves of books would need to be written to fully explore the ways the internet has caused creative destruction in the world. Our discussion inevitably leaves out many of the internet's important impacts. Instead, we describe some examples of creative destruction that directly demonstrate the internet's cultural, social, and political effects. We first discuss some cultural and social effects together, as these two categories tend to overlap and rarely lend themselves to strict divisions. Then we discuss some effects that are likely to affect political institutions.

Our discussion of the political consequences of creative destruction enabled by the internet is important to the overall narrative of this book for two reasons. First, the political consequences unleashed by creative destruction from the internet underscore the potential for innovations and the creative destruction that results from them to radically transform society. In this way, the internet's political consequences mirror the printing press's role in the Reformation. Second, the fact that the political consequences of the internet seem highly disruptive and uncertain underscores the need to protect innovation and creative destruction from their detractors. Otherwise, defenders of the status quo who feel threatened by creative destruction will have the power to contain the capacity to resist change and slow creative destruction, which can slow economic growth and flourishing in human welfare. The severity of the consequences of creative destruction, and the resistance creative destruction can create, underscore the need to mitigate the effects of destruction on people's lives while simultaneously fostering creation.

To begin with a relatively benign example of the internet's creative destruction, let's return to where we last left off in the example of Netflix—the dawning of the age of streaming. Streaming has led to cultural transformation in both the production and consumption of entertainment, especially with respect to TV episodes, which tend to be shorter than movies. With access to entire back catalogs of TV episodes, consumers can now easily watch their old and new favorites, sometimes leading us to binge-watch entire seasons of shows in single sittings. We tell ourselves it is just so easy to click on the next episode to continue the story. Besides, it can take as little as 30 minutes or less to watch another episode.

The popularity of online video streaming has led to both the creation of new types of writing and new ways of watching TV shows. On the production side, this varying length of episodes is one of the consequences of streaming. No longer beholden to commercial breaks and traditional TV time slots, writers and directors have responded by producing episodes of varying lengths depending on the narrative demands of the series and the episode at hand. The release from these constraints has fostered greater creative freedom. The lack of commercial breaks means producers and directors have more time to develop particular plot lines during an episode;

instead of an hour episode including 45 minutes of content and 15 minutes of commercials, an hour episode can include a full hour's worth of content. The result of these production changes has been more variety and, in many cases, higher quality of shows to satisfy more viewers and more varied tastes—and has helped fuel the demand for additional content. That demand has been met by a flurry of new entrants producing TV shows, further contributing to the dynamism of today's TV landscape.

Streaming TV shows makes up a small slice of the larger e-commerce sector the internet created. The physical, digital, and virtual economies have all been shaped by the internet. From Amazon and eBay for physical goods to YouTube and Netflix for online content, the internet has created much with regard to commerce. What has been destroyed are typically older ways of doing business that failed to embrace the internet or were simply overwhelmed by the rapid ascendancy of all things internet. Think mom-and-pop retailers unable to compete against Amazon and exiting the market. Or outdoors neighborhood play declining as children's play moves online to the virtual worlds of gaming. Indeed, one of the main casualties from the internet's creative destruction seems to be the growing disconnect between us and our physical surroundings, as we move ever deeper into digital and virtual realities.

Substituting the digital and virtual worlds of entertainment for the world of work seems to be a greater problem for young men. The flow of satisfaction many young men derive from watching YouTube, playing video games, posting on social media, or viewing pornography appears to outweigh the benefits of joining the labor market. Analysis of time diary data confirms that the value of these online leisure activities has contributed to the drop in hours worked by young men.[5] Young men's exiting the labor market raises all sorts of challenges both for them and for society at large. From the lack of marriage prospects to decreased human capital accumulation and lifetime earnings to sluggish productivity growth, the movement toward living more of life online may create a drag on economic growth. Unemployed men also frequently engage in crime and conflict.

The internet's creative destruction is also transforming social ties and courtship rituals, as dating apps have become a primary tool people use to form romantic relationships. Dating websites drastically reduce the costs of solving what economists refer to as matching problems. A matching problem describes any situation in which two parties attempt to align, or match, their preferences in a transaction. The canonical example in economic theory is when an employer and employee attempt to match in the labor market. Employers demand a set of skills to fill a particular job, while potential employees who embody those skills look for work. Employers and employees lack perfect information about each other, so they engage in costly search in the labor market to find the best match.

Any mechanism that decreases search costs to facilitate better matching outcomes can make the market more efficient by reducing its transaction costs. Economists use the term "transaction cost" to describe any cost to making a trade in a market. Reducing transaction costs benefits market participants and leads to better outcomes, like increased consumption and production, and thus greater economic growth. Innovation frequently reduces transaction costs, much as dating sites do for the dating and marriage markets. As seen in Chapter 5, Uber also reduced transaction costs between passengers and drivers wanting to transact to produce a ride.

In the case of dating websites, users create profiles containing information about themselves and what qualities they are seeking in a partner. The site's matching algorithm then matches profiles to suggest potential dates. These dates then lead to romantic relationships, couple formation, and then eventually marriage. The internet's creative destruction is, thus, transforming the ways in which one of the most fundamental units of society comes about. What is created is presumably better matches, and what is destroyed is the old way of matching.

But there are numerous other consequences, the most important of which appears to be an increase in assortative rather than random mating. In practice, assortative mating has meant that people with similar skill and income levels are more frequently being matched.[6] Whereas it used to be more common for, say, a schoolteacher to match with a doctor, now a doctor matches with a lawyer. Assortative mating can exacerbate inequality, as doctor-lawyer couples earn more income and accumulate more wealth than, say, schoolteacher-plumber couples. Higher inequality can then generate political conflict between high- and low-income groups. So what seems like a great new way to meet the love of your life can have deep cultural, social, and political implications through the creative destruction it entails.

We encountered a similar phenomenon in the case of Netflix's search algorithm, as your viewing history influences which videos show up on your feed—a form of matching and a vastly different experience from random browsing at Blockbuster. Matching is a key feature of many websites, from

Amazon and YouTube to eBay and Etsy. Matching shows up in these sites' algorithms much like it does on Netflix—the site's technology matches your browsing history with new suggestions.

But the internet also facilitates matching through simple search, as in Google or any search feature on Amazon, eBay, or other websites. Searching has transformed buying habits. The main benefit is, of course, that we can seek out products exactly, or at least close to, matching our specifications. Etsy is a great example. Etsy mostly hosts sale listings from small businesses, including many small-scale artisans, around the world. The listings include seemingly every imaginable small consumer item. The joy of searching on Etsy is that you can locate special items that are hard to find and may even be handcrafted just for you.

Unfortunately, though not frequently acknowledged, search can also have its downsides. Consumers now know they can find the perfect match in a product they seek and may come to expect to find a perfect match every time. Being unable to find that perfect match can become frustrating for some, leading to unrealistic expectations and large amounts of time spent searching. Consumers who care less about the perfect match may not face this downside, which suggests search's downside affects consumers differently.

Matching on the internet is not confined to consumer products. Matching helps people of similar interests connect and
build communities not restricted by geography, as the earlier
example of the Lego YouTube videos attests.

Reddit is an even better example. Reddit is a discussion
website where users submit content that is then organized
into different communities or "subreddits." Reddit's thematic
rabbit holes are seemingly never ending. Consider Lego. Typ-
ing in "Lego" to the Reddit search bar returns hundreds of
subreddits.[7] Of course, there is r/lego (subreddits are named
"r/" followed by the title) with over 1.1 million users, which is
the main Lego subreddit. But then there are others to satisfy
any Lego interest: r/legodeal (over 96,000 thousands members) consists of users posting Lego sales from various sellers;
r/LegoStorage (over 22,000 members) is for users to show
off their Lego storage solutions; r/legoRockets (over 4,000
members) is for users who want to showcase their brick-built
rockets; r/legocastles (over 9,000 members) is where fans of
the popular Lego castle theme congregate; and so on. Can't
find what you're looking for? Then create your own subreddit
and begin to build your community. Reddit provides limitless
opportunities for community building in the virtual world.

Labor markets have also benefited from closer matching
of employers and employees through such online services as

LinkedIn. LinkedIn allows employers to post job vacancies. Workers who have profiles on LinkedIn can communicate with other workers and employers and apply for vacancies. A recent randomized training program showed that workers receiving training on how to use LinkedIn experienced a 10 percent higher employment rate after the program compared with those who received no training.[8] Social media, like Facebook and Twitter, are another example of matching, as your liking and reposting curate the information coming across your screen to better fit your interests.

However, creative destruction from social media also has its downsides. Critics of social media point to how cultivating your own personal stream leads to the siloing of information and the deepening of confirmation bias, which is when we selectively interpret information to support our prior beliefs. Taken to an extreme, confirmation bias can close us off to new ideas and make it harder to cooperate with others who do not share our beliefs. Our personalized information silos may weaken our shared ties, fracturing public spaces in the process and increasing political polarization. Insofar as polarization drives political turmoil and dysfunction, the creative destruction of social media may be wiping away a more civil and cooperative type of governance and fostering the emergence of more discord. Political polarization and dysfunction can be bad for economic growth, as institutional rules of governance oscillate wildly when political power changes hands. Institutional instability is bad for business.

The final political consequences of the creative destruction unleashed by the internet, especially by social media, are not yet known. Only the benefits of time will allow us to fully appreciate the internet's consequences, as with the printing press's role in the Reformation. One hypothesis that appears promising, however, is the role of democratized information in the so-called revolt of the public put forth by former CIA media analyst and author Martin Gurri.[9] Gurri's analysis of the relationship between the internet and our current political structures unfolds as follows: The internet has led to the democratization of information, as far larger amounts of information can spread around the world quickly and easily. This democratization of access to information threatens the prevailing narratives about the world, such as those put forward by elites in established media, the corporate world, and government. At the same time, better access to information allows us to learn more about elites and reveals their faults to us, damaging their reputations and undermining their authority. The more information diffuses throughout the internet, the more questionable the political status quo appears. Individuals with access to the democratized information pose an existential threat to government authority. The danger is that governments can respond with repression, which then further increases the public's desire to subvert established authority, leading to a downward spiral of political disintegration.

Gurri sees many such examples since the rise of social media—such as the Arab Spring, Brexit, and the election of Donald Trump—to support his hypothesis about democratized information and the revolt of the public. To prevent political disintegration, both the public and the government need to learn to cooperate with each other better in the new world of democratized information. The public needs to expect less from government and to gain a better understanding of how it works. Government officials, meanwhile, need to promise less and exert less control over people's lives. If this new state of cooperation were to emerge, it would be another example of how creative destruction can initially disrupt the status quo but then over time lead to an overall better outcome for society as a whole.

Gurri's vision of the internet's consequences sounds eerily similar to the role of the printing press in spreading information that helped undermine the unquestioned authority of the Catholic Church. Both innovations fundamentally transformed how we communicate with one another. As Gurri's hypothesis reminds us, the internet's consequences for the future may be just as significant as the Reformation, the Enlightenment, and the Scientific Revolution.

Artificial Intelligence and the Future of Creative Destruction

Economists often focus on creative destruction's process of innovation and its direct economic consequences, but that is far from the full picture. As we have argued throughout this chapter, innovation and creative destruction contain the potential to remake all aspects of our world. We may not be able to foresee the ultimate consequences of an innovation as it first begins to be adopted, but the history of innovation and creative destruction teaches us to anticipate that the consequences may be profound not only for the economy but for the wider cultural, social, and political landscape. With this in mind, we conclude by briefly considering a technology that has been making big leaps forward during the time we were writing this book—namely, artificial intelligence, or AI.

AI refers to intelligence demonstrated by machines, as opposed to, say, human intelligence. AI is already embedded in many technologies we use today, some of which we have encountered in this chapter. The matching and search algorithms of Netflix, YouTube, Amazon, and other websites are examples of AI applications. AI helps power self-driving cars, like Tesla's autopilot feature, and voice recognition devices, like Amazon's Alexa. Examples of AI are many and varied and have undoubtedly led to creative destruction. But for the purposes of this discussion, we will focus on what most people at the time of this writing think of when they think of AI—ChatGPT.

ChatGPT is a generative—GPT stands for "generative pretrained transformer"—or creative AI tool developed by OpenAI, an AI research lab based in the United States. The technology on which ChatGPT is based is called a large language model (LLM). There are many LLM-based technologies, but ChatGPT is the industry leader—for now—so we use it as an example. ChatGPT is a software application that essentially mimics human conversation. A user types in a prompt, such as "Who was Joseph Schumpeter?" or "What is creative destruction?," and ChatGPT responds with an answer. The potential uses of ChatGPT—answering simple questions like those just posed, improving computer code, summarizing longer writings, answering homework questions, writing essays, developing business materials like marketing pitches, and writing poetry and music—appear to be limitless. The potential of ChatGPT has not gone unnoticed, and its user base has exploded, setting an internet record as the consumer application reaching 100 million active users in the shortest amount of time.[10]

What is clear from the early days of ChatGPT is that it and similar AI technologies possess the capacity for significant creation and destruction. The creation side of the ledger is obvious, even as it is not yet fully known. ChatGPT enables white-collar workers to achieve far higher levels of productivity—the example of writing and refining computer code being a good one. As we saw in Chapter 2, higher productivity can boost economic growth and increase living standards. As of this writing, it is too early for the destruction side of the ledger to have been realized, but the world may not have to wait long for the effects of ChatGPT's destructive potential to be felt.

Just as ChatGPT makes white-collar workers more productive, it also means fewer white-collar workers are required to complete any one task. We can think of these changes as being similar to the effects of automation and international trade on the nature of blue-collar work and the number of blue-collar workers required to perform specific tasks. ChatGPT will have distributional consequences among white-collar workers. Those who are able to embrace the new technology and use it as a tool will see increased productivity and job prospects, whereas those workers slow to adopt the technology or unable to use it altogether will face diminished job prospects and possibly unemployment. Let go of their jobs, white-collar workers will join the churn of labor markets we encountered in Chapter 1, as jobs are ceaselessly created and destroyed. Schumpeter's gale will continue to blow.

As we have seen in the case of the printing press, the disruptions from these changes can be so severe that they can lead to backlash. In effect, creative destruction is always sowing the seeds of its own destruction—and at the same time, creative destruction is continuously opening new paths for creating new forms of working and living. AI will present similar opportunities and challenges. If economic growth and prosperity are to flourish, creative destruction must always have its defenders.

Conclusion

Joseph Schumpeter would recognize our world. He was born at a time when the last visages of feudal Europe were being swept away by the creative destruction unleashed by relentless modern economic growth. As a boy, a young man, and then a rising star in the world of professional economics, his life in techno-romantic Vienna—that period of Viennese history when the clash between technological change and capitalism, on the one hand, and imperialism and aristocracy, on the other, was on such vivid display—exposed him to the incessant industrial mutation transforming the society around him, consistent with his vision of a dynamic world. By identifying creative destruction as the essential fact about capitalism, he tapped into a truth about both his world and ours: creative destruction, fueled by innovation, powers the internal dynamics of capitalism, incessantly destroying the existing economic structures and creating new ones.

Today, we encounter Schumpeter's vision all around us. We see creative destruction at work when entrepreneurs aspire to remake how we watch movies at home. Netflix enters the market, leaving Blockbuster a mere memory in its wake. A woman wants to make a better life for herself and her family and struggles against overwhelming odds to bring her Miracle Mop to market. That mop changes how all of us clean our floors today. Young tech entrepreneurs launch social media companies like Facebook and Twitter with hopes of bringing the world closer together and giving all of us a voice in shaping the future, but, in the process, political earthquakes shake the foundations of society, the new fault lines of which remain uncertain. Creative destruction continued to remake our world even amid the COVID-19 pandemic, as once little-known companies like Zoom emerged to be market leaders in response to government lockdowns and quarantines to usher in a new age of remote work.

Life in a world of creative destruction is chaotic but good and always improving. Creative destruction is part of long-run economic growth that built the modern world, with all of its enrichment and life-sustaining innovations. A world of low growth, and low amounts of creative destruction, leads to stagnation and impoverishment compared with what is possible when entrepreneurship and risk taking are unleashed. Creative destruction promises a potentially limitless future of prosperity. We do not know what the economy of the future will look like, but it will be beneficial if we arrive there on a wave of creative destruction. Creative destruction always contains the potential seeds of its own destruction, as well as the solutions to the disruptions it creates in the process.

We have only written an introduction to the topic of creative destruction. Interested readers wanting to learn more should begin by reading both of Schumpeter's classics: *The Theory of Economic Development* and *Capitalism, Socialism and Democracy*. Both books contain much that is essential for understanding our modern world, and Schumpeter remains a compelling thinker whose writing speaks to us with insights that continue to shed light on contemporary issues. As we have written elsewhere, Francis Bacon's advice applies to Schumpeter's books: "Some books are to be tasted, others to be swallowed, and some few to be chewed and digested. . . ."[1] At that time, we were writing specifically about *Capitalism, Socialism and Democracy*, but the same is true of *The Theory of*

Economic Development. Both are among the few books requiring chewing and digesting.[2]

Moreover, we encourage readers to adopt and share Schumpeter's vision. View the world through the lens of creative destruction. What do you see? How does the world look different? Does it change your understanding of innovation and the incessant change innovation causes? What are you doing to foster more economic growth? What about those hurt by creative destruction's chaos? Dynamism, not stasis— that is Schumpeter's vision of creative destruction.

Acknowledgments

We thank the Center for the Study of Capitalism at Wake Forest University for its generous financial support in freeing up John Dalton's time for writing this book.

We also thank everyone at the Cato Institute who diligently worked alongside us to make this book a reality. Paul Matzko and his team of reviewers accepted our original encyclopedia entry on creative destruction for Libertarianism.org, which paved the way for a book proposal. We are grateful for Ivan Osorio's editing, which led to numerous improvements of the manuscript. Grant Babcock and Jonathan Fortier also read the manuscript and gave us useful comments. Eleanor O'Connor kept everyone organized and on track throughout the writing and publication process. We also thank copy-editor Joanne Platt and proofreader Kate Hall of Publications

Professionals LLC and the typesetter for bringing the manuscript into its final form.

John would like to thank his wife, Tina, who is the source of so much positive creative destruction in his life.

Andrew would like to thank his family for their support and John for the friendship and mentorship over the years.

Notes

Chapter 1

1. The RIAA database currently resides at https://www.riaa.com/u-s-sales -database/. The data appearing in this book were downloaded in May 2021. We thank Koleman Strumpf for pointing these data out to us.

2. The categories in Figure 1.1 are constructed from the RIAA database as follows: "8-tracks" is the RIAA category 8-track; "Vinyl records" is the RIAA categories LP/EP and Vinyl Single; "Cassettes" is the RIAA categories Cassette and Cassette Single; "Compact discs" is the RIAA categories CD and CD Single; and "Downloads" is the RIAA categories Download Album and Download Single.

3. The "Streaming" category in Figure 1.2 consists of the RIAA categories Paid Subscriptions and On-Demand Streaming.

4. Randy Alfred, "Dec. 16, 1770: Beethoven's Birth in Bonn Leads to Longer CDs," *Wired*, December 16, 2010.

5. U.S. Census Bureau, Business Dynamics Statistics website, https://www .census.gov/programs-surveys/bds.html.

6. Joseph A. Schumpeter, *Capitalism, Socialism and Democracy* (New York: Harper & Row, 1950), p. 83.

7. Schumpeter, *Capitalism*, p. 84.

8. Deirdre N. McCloskey, *Bourgeois Equality: How Ideas, Not Capital or Institutions, Enriched the World* (Chicago: University of Chicago Press, 2016).

9. Joseph A. Schumpeter, *The Theory of Economic Development: An Inquiry into Profits, Capital, Credit, Interest, and the Business Cycle*, trans. Redvers Opie (Cambridge, MA: Harvard University Press, 1934), p. 64.

10. Robert Loring Allen, *Opening Doors: The Life and Work of Joseph Schumpeter*, vol. 1, *Europe* (New Brunswick, NJ: Transaction Publishers, 1991), p. 18–22.

11. Thomas K. McCraw, *Prophet of Innovation: Joseph Schumpeter and Creative Destruction* (Cambridge, MA: Belknap Press of Harvard University Press, 2007), p. 34. McCraw uses the phrase "techno-romantic" to describe the Vienna of Schumpeter's time.

12. McCraw, *Prophet of Innovation*, pp. 98–101.

13. McCraw, *Prophet of Innovation*, p. 14.

14. Carl E. Schorske, *Fin-de-Siècle Vienna: Politics and Culture* (New York: Knopf, 1985), p. 79.

15. Schorske, *Fin-de-Siècle Vienna*, p. 226.

16. Schorske, *Fin-de-Siècle Vienna*, p. 225–73.

17. Schorske, *Fin-de-Siècle Vienna*, p. 225–73.

18. When economists participating in a survey were asked, "Are there any economic thinkers of the twentieth century and now deceased whom you regard with great respect, admiration, or reverence?," Schumpeter came in as the fifth most popular choice. See William L. Davis et al., "Economics Professors' Favorite Economic Thinkers, Journals, and Blogs (along with Party and Policy Views)," *Econ Journal Watch* 8, no. 2 (2011): 126–46. Similarly, academic citations to Schumpeter continue to grow over time, even outstripping those to John Maynard Keynes. See Arthur M. Diamond, "Schumpeter vs. Keynes: 'In the Long Run Not All of Us Are Dead,'" *Journal of the History of Economic Thought* 31, no. 4 (2009): 531–41; and John T. Dalton and Lillian R. Gaeto, "Schumpeter vs. Keynes Redux: 'Still Not Dead,'" *Southern Economic Journal* 89, no. 2 (2020): 569–92.

19. For a recent history of the Austrian school of economics, including its early years in Vienna in which Schumpeter appears, see Janek Wasserman, *The Marginal Revolutionaries: How Austrian Economists Fought the War of Ideas* (New Haven, CT: Yale University Press, 2019). For a contemporary overview of Austrian economics in general, see Steven Horwitz, *Austrian Economics: An Introduction* (Washington: Cato Institute, 2020).

20. Wasserman, *Marginal Revolutionaries*, p. 86.

21. McCraw, *Prophet of Innovation*, p. 45.

22. Joseph A. Schumpeter, *Ten Great Economists: From Marx to Keynes* (New York: Oxford University Press, 1951), pp. 143–44.

23. Wasserman, *Marginal Revolutionaries*, p. 86.

24. See the epigraph in Wolfgang F. Stolper, *Joseph Alois Schumpeter: The Public Life of a Private Man* (Princeton, NJ: Princeton University Press, 1994).

Chapter 2

1. For an overview of how GDP statistics came about, see Diane Coyle, *GDP: A Brief but Affectionate History* (Princeton, NJ: Princeton University Press, 2015).

2. This story about Marshall's development as an economist was popularized by John Maynard Keynes in his biography of Marshall. See John M. Keynes, *The Collected Writings of John Maynard Keynes: Essays in Biography*, vol. 10 (Cambridge, UK: Royal Economic Society, 1971), p. 171.

3. Robert E. Lucas Jr., "On the Mechanics of Economic Development," *Journal of Monetary Economics* 22, no. 1 (1988): 3–42.

4. For a history of growth theory, including Lucas's contributions, see David Warsh, *Knowledge and the Wealth of Nations: A Story of Economic Discovery* (New York: W. W. Norton, 2006).

5. Lucas, "Economic Development," p. 3.

6. Ramgopal Agarwala et al., *World Development Report 1983* (Washington: World Bank, 1983).

7. Lucas, "Economic Development," p. 3.

8. Lucas, "Economic Development," p. 4.

9. Lucas, "Economic Development," p. 5 (emphasis in original).

10. According to David Warsh, a journalist and author who has written exten-sively on the economics profession, this passage by Lucas became one of the most quoted by an economist since John Maynard Keynes's "the ideas of economists and political philosophers . . . are more powerful than is commonly understood." See Warsh, *Knowledge and the Wealth of Nations*, p. 247.

11. For a recent overview of the varied causes of economic growth, see Mark Koyama and Jared Rubin, *How the World Became Rich: The Historical Origins of Economic Growth* (Cambridge, UK: Polity Press, 2022).

12. Jagdish Bhagwati and Arvind Panagariya, *Why Growth Matters: How Economic Growth in India Reduced Poverty and the Lessons for Other Developing Countries* (New York: PublicAffairs, 2013).

13. McCloskey argues her case throughout an impressive trilogy of books: *The Bourgeois Virtues: Ethics for an Age of Commerce* (Chicago: University of Chicago Press, 2006); *Bourgeois Dignity: Why Economics Can't Explain the Modern World* (Chicago: University of Chicago Press, 2010); and *Bourgeois Equality: How Ideas, Not Capital or Institutions, Enriched the World* (Chicago: University of Chicago Press, 2016).

14. Deirdre N. McCloskey and Art Carden, *Leave Me Alone and I'll Make You Rich: How the Bourgeois Deal Enriched the World* (Chicago: University of Chicago Press, 2020).

15. The data are from Angus Maddison, "Historical Statistics of the World Economy: 1–2008 AD," 2010, https://www.rug.nl/ggdc/historicaldevelopment /maddison/releases/maddison-database-2010. The Maddison data are well known to economists, and the 2010 iteration was the final release by Maddison before his death.

16. Big Mac Index, *The Economist*, https://www.economist.com/big-mac-index.

17. "Western Europe" in Figure 2.2 refers to the category of 12 western European countries in Maddison's database: Austria, Belgium, Denmark, Finland, France, Germany, Italy, the Netherlands, Norway, Sweden, Switzerland, and the United Kingdom.

18. The Maddison data contain estimates for regions and countries. In this case, yes, there would be no United States politically in year 1, but it would be an estimate for this region. The problem of political changes to geographic regions is inherent whenever long-run growth numbers are being considered.

19. This population figure for Africa in 2021 comes from the World Bank's *World Development Indicators*, https://databank.worldbank.org/source/world -development-indicators.

20. The economist Tyler Cowen has written extensively about the rise of the complacent class in the case of the United States. See Tyler Cowen, *The Complacent Class: The Self-Defeating Quest for the American Dream* (New York: St. Martin's Press, 2017).

21. See, for example, Tyler Cowen, *The Great Stagnation: How America Ate All the Low-Hanging Fruit of Modern History, Got Sick, and Will (Eventually) Feel Better* (New York: Dutton, 2011). See also Robert J. Gordon, *The Rise and Fall of American Growth: The U.S. Standard of Living since the Civil War* (Princeton, NJ: Princeton University Press, 2016).

22. Joseph A. Schumpeter, *Capitalism, Socialism and Democracy* (New York: Harper & Row, 1950), p. 67.

23. Schumpeter, *Capitalism*, p. 123.

24. Schumpeter, *Capitalism*, p. 124.

25. Schumpeter, *Capitalism*, p. 126.

26. Tyler Cowen, *Stubborn Attachments: A Vision for a Society of Free, Prosperous, and Responsible Individuals* (San Francisco: Stripe Press, 2018), p. 5 (emphasis in original).

Chapter 3

1. Joseph A. Schumpeter, *Capitalism, Socialism and Democracy* (New York: Harper & Row, 1950), p. 83.

2. Ludwig von Mises, *Socialism: An Economic and Sociological Analysis* (New York: Macmillan, 1936).

3. Deirdre N. McCloskey, *The Bourgeois Virtues: Ethics for an Age of Commerce* (Chicago: University of Chicago Press, 2006); *Bourgeois Dignity: Why Economics*

Can't Explain the Modern World (Chicago: University of Chicago Press, 2010); and *Bourgeois Equality: How Ideas, Not Capital or Institutions, Enriched the World* (Chicago: University of Chicago Press, 2016).

4. This particular formulation of McCloskey's Bourgeois Deal is quoted directly from page 572 of John T. Dalton and Andrew J. Logan, "A Vision for a Dynamic World: Reading *Capitalism, Socialism and Democracy* for Today," *Independent Review* 24, no. 4 (2020): 567–77.

5. Philippe Aghion and Gilles Saint-Paul, "Virtues of Bad Times: Interaction between Productivity Growth and Economic Fluctuations," *Macroeconomic Dynamics* 2, no. 3 (1998): 322–44.

6. Steven J. Davis and John Haltiwanger, "Gross Job Creation and Destruction: Microeconomic Evidence and Macroeconomic Implications," in *NBER Macroeconomics Annual*, vol. 5, ed. Olivier Jean Blanchard and Stanley Fischer (Cambridge, MA: National Bureau of Economic Research, 1990), pp. 123–86.

7. Schumpeter, *Capitalism*, p. 84.

8. Ian Klaus, *Forging Capitalism: Rogues, Swindlers, Frauds, and the Rise of Modern Finance* (New Haven, CT: Yale University Press, 2014).

9. Interestingly, research in organizational studies has found that firms that obtain resources through fraudulent means are less likely to pursue technically significant innovations. This suggests that they are more likely to face technological obsolescence and fall victim to creative destruction. See Yanbo Wang, Toby Stuart, and Jizhen Li, "Fraud and Innovation," *Administrative Science Quarterly* 66, no. 2 (2021): 267–97.

10. McCloskey, *Bourgeois Virtues*.

11. Alex Tabarrok, "The Invisible Hand Increases Trust, Cooperation, and Universal Moral Action," *Marginal Revolution* (blog), October 8, 2022.

12. Baron de Montesquieu, *The Spirit of the Laws*, vol. 1 (New York: Classics of Liberty Library, 1991), p. 1.

13. Voltaire was making this observation in his *Philosophical Dictionary*, which can be found at the Liberty Fund's Online Library of Liberty.

14. See, for example, more recent papers: Joseph Henrich et al., "In Search of Homo Economicus: Behavioral Experiments in 15 Small-Scale Societies,"

American Economic Review 91, no. 2 (2001): 73–78; Delia Baldassarri, "Market Integration Accounts for Local Variation in Generalized Altruism in a Nationwide Lost-Letter Experiment," *Proceedings of the National Academy of Sciences* 117, no. 6 (2020): 2858–63; Omar Al-Ubaydli et al., "The Causal Effect of Market Priming on Trust: An Experimental Investigation Using Randomized Control," *PLOS One* 8, no. 3 (2013): e55968; and Gustav Agneman and Esther Chevrot-Bianco, "Market Participation and Moral Decision-Making: Experimental Evidence from Greenland," *Economic Journal* 133, no. 650 (2023): 537–81.

15. Paul Starobin and Catherine Belton, "Gazprom: Russia's Enron," Bloomberg, February 18, 2022.

16. Marielle Eudes, "Gazprom Audit Leads to 'Russia's Enron,'" *Baltic Times*, April 18, 2002.

17. Nicholas Hirst, "Commission Charges Gazprom," *Politico*, April 22, 2015.

18. George Stigler, *Memoirs of an Unregulated Economist* (New York: Basic Books, 1985), p. 101.

Chapter 4

1. Deirdre N. McCloskey, "The Great Enrichment: A Humanistic and Social Scientific Account," *Social Science History* 40, no. 4 (2016): 583–98.

2. Joseph A. Schumpeter, *The Theory of Economic Development: An Inquiry into Profits, Capital, Credit, Interest, and the Business Cycle*, trans. Redvers Opie (Cambridge, MA: Harvard University Press, 1934), pp. 57–94.

3. Newsweek Special Edition, "The Story of Steve Jobs, Xerox, and Who Really Invented the Personal Computer," *Newsweek*, March 19, 2016.

4. Schumpeter, *Economic Development*, p. 66.

5. Bruce A. Blonigen and Justin R. Pierce, "Evidence for the Effects of Mergers on Market Power and Efficiency," National Bureau of Economic Research Working Paper no. 22750, October 2016.

6. Schumpeter, *Economic Development*, p. 74. The use of the word "ephor" in Schumpeter's quotation may be obscure to the modern reader, but it would have been better known to Schumpeter's contemporaries with their classical educations.

The ephors were a council consisting of five members of ancient Spartan society. They held a range of powers in Sparta that enabled them to influence the direction of society at any given point in time. What Schumpeter means is that bankers, through their allocation of credit, oversee the direction of the economy. Bankers act as a guiding force in the economy, much like the Spartan ephors in their own society.

7. Schumpeter, *Economic Development*, p. 86.

8. Schumpeter, *Economic Development*, p. 93.

9. John T. Dalton and Andrew J. Logan, "Using the Movie *Joy* to Teach Innovation and Entrepreneurship," *Journal of Economic Education* 51, no. 3–4 (2020): 287–96.

10. Clayton M. Christensen, Scott D. Anthony, and Erik A. Roth, *Seeing What's Next: Using Theories of Innovation to Predict Industry Change* (Cambridge, MA: Harvard Business School Press, 2004).

11. We recognize that at the time of this writing Musk is a divisive figure, especially with regard to his takeover of Twitter (now called X). From the lens of Schumpeter's theory, however, Musk is an exemplary example of how the lines between entrepreneurs and incumbent firms can blur. Moreover, we should point out that many of Musk's loudest critics, such as those in traditional media outlets, are those under the greatest threat of competition from Twitter, especially when it comes to controlling the flow of information people consume. Twitter is one of the forces behind Schumpeter's gale in the media industry and is contributing to the democratization of information. At the same time, its recent struggles show that it is also not immune to creative destruction. We will expand on this point later in Chapter 6 when discussing the work of Martin Gurri.

12. "Luddite," *Encyclopedia Britannica*, accessed September 13, 2022.

13. Eric J. Hobsbawm, "The Machine Breakers," *Past & Present* 1, no. 1 (1952): 57–70.

Chapter 5

1. Matt Phillips and Roberto A. Ferdman, "A Brief, Illustrated History of Blockbuster, Which Is Closing the Last of Its US Stores," *Quartz*, November 6, 2013.

2. For example, Marc Randolph, *That Will Never Work: The Birth of Netflix and the Amazing Life of an Idea* (New York: Little, Brown, 2019); *Netflix vs. the World*, directed by Shawn Cauthen, written by Gina Keating, featuring Marc Randolf, John Antioco, and Shane Evangelist, 2020, Amazon Prime Video; and Chunka Mui, "How Netflix Innovates and Wins," *Forbes*, March 17, 2011.

3. Andy Ash, "The Rise and Fall of Blockbuster and How It's Surviving with Just One Store Left," *Business Insider*, August 12, 2020.

4. *The Last Blockbuster*, directed by Taylor Morden, written by Zeke Kamm, featuring Lauren Lapkus, Tom Casey, and Kevin Smith, 2020, 1091 Pictures.

5. History.com Editorial Staff, "This Day in History: The First Blockbuster Opens," History.com, October 20, 2021.

6. Natasha Lavender, "The Untold Truth of Blockbuster," *Grunge*, January 12, 2022.

7. Byron Acohido, "When the Party's Over," *Inc.*, July 1, 1987.

8. Frank Olito and Alex Bitter, "The Rise and Fall of Blockbuster," *Business Insider*, August 20, 2023.

9. Associated Press, "Video Industry Hopes Latest Hits Will Help Summer Rentals Rebound," May 26, 1992.

10. Associated Press, "Video Industry Hopes."

11. Associated Press, "Video Industry Hopes."

12. Christopher Harress, "The Sad End of Blockbuster Video: The Onetime $5 Billion Company Is Being Liquidated as Competition from Online Giants Netflix and Hulu Prove All Too Much for the Iconic Brand," *International Business Times*, December 5, 2013.

13. *The Last Blockbuster*, 2020.

14. Geraldine Fabrikant, "Attack of the Disruptive Disc; Sales of DVD's Are Challenging the Business of Renting Movies," *New York Times*, April 16, 2001.

15. Edward J. Epstein, "Hollywood's New Zombie," *Slate*, January 9, 2006.

16. Epstein, "Hollywood's New Zombie."

17. Michael Liedtke and Mae Anderson, "Blockbuster Tries to Rewrite Script in Bankruptcy," *Boston Globe*, July 23, 2006.

18. Olito and Bitter, "Rise and Fall of Blockbuster."

19. Minda Zetlin, "Blockbuster Could Have Bought Netflix for $50 Million, but the CEO Thought It Was a Joke," *Inc.*, September 20, 2019.

20. Billboard Staff, "Blockbuster Eliminates Late Fees," *Billboard*, December 14, 2004.

21. Lorenza Munoz, "Blockbuster to Halt Late Fees, but There's a Catch," *Los Angeles Times*, December 15, 2004.

22. Rob Frappier, "After Major Losses, Blockbuster Brings Back Late Fees," *Screen Rant*, March 4, 2010.

23. "A Timeline: The Blockbuster Life Cycle," *Forbes*, April 7, 2011.

24. Lorenza Munoz, "Blockbuster Sued over Late Fee Claims," *Los Angeles Times*, February 19, 2005.

25. John Lippman and James Bates, "Viacom, Blockbuster Unveil Surprise Merger," *Los Angeles Times*, January 8, 1994.

26. "A Timeline," *Forbes*.

27. Nicole Sperling, "Long Before 'Netflix and Chill,' He Was the Netflix C.E.O.," *New York Times*, September 15, 2019.

28. Randolph, *The Birth of Netflix*, p. 27.

29. Randolph, *The Birth of Netflix*, p. 78.

30. Randolph, *The Birth of Netflix*, p. 13.

31. Randolph, *The Birth of Netflix*.

32. Stephanie Gandel, "How Blockbuster Failed at Failing," *Time,* October 17, 2010.

33. Joseph A. Schumpeter, *The Theory of Economic Development: An Inquiry into Profits, Capital, Credit, Interest, and the Business Cycle*, trans. Redvers Opie (Cambridge, MA: Harvard University Press, 1934), p. 70.

34. Randolph, *The Birth of Netflix*, p. 48.

35. Randolph, *The Birth of Netflix*.

36. Silicon Valley Business Journal, "NetFlix Garners $30 Million Investment," July 11, 1999.

37. "Netflix Announces First Quarter 2003 Ending Subscribers of 1,052,000, Up 74% over the Prior Year," Netflix news release, April 1, 2003.

38. Associated Press, "Netflix Reaches Milestone with Delivery of 1 Billionth DVD," *Victoria Advocate*, February 26, 2007.

39. Liedtke and Anderson, "Blockbuster Tries to Rewrite Script."

40. "A Timeline," *Forbes.*

41. Alexis C. Madrigal, "The Electric Taxi Company You Could Have Called in 2011," *The Atlantic*, March 15, 2011.

42. Lawrence Van Gelder, "Medallion Limits Stem from the 30's," *New York Times*, May 11, 1996.

43. Ironically, this first effort at instituting a medallion system failed after it was discovered that the Parmelee Company, New York's biggest taxicab operator, had paid a substantial bribe to Mayor Jimmy Walker to help push the proposal through.

44. Van Gelder, "Medallion Limits." The inflation adjustment used here was calculated from the U.S. Bureau of Labor Statistics' CPI Inflation Calculator.

45. Lizzie Widdicombe, "Thin Yellow Line," *New Yorker*, April 11, 2011.

46. Brian O'Connell, "History of Uber: Timeline and Facts," *TheStreet*, July 23, 2019.

47. O'Connell, "History of Uber."

48. O'Connell, "History of Uber."

49. "Uber Announces Results for Fourth Quarter and Full Year," Securities and Exchange Commission news release, February 6, 2020.

50. Julian Birkinshaw, "Uber—A Story of Creative Destruction," *Forbes*, October 16, 2017.

51. Michael M. Grynbaum, "2 Taxi Medallions Sell for $1 Million Each," *New York Times*, October 20, 2011.

52. Grynbaum, "2 Taxi Medallions Sell for $1 Million Each."

53. Matt Flemengeimer, "De Blasio Administration Dropping Plan for Uber Cap, for Now," *New York Times*, July 22, 2015.

54. Data Team, "Substitutes or Complements?," *The Economist*, August 10, 2015.

55. Data Team, "Substitutes or Complements?"

56. Carl Bialik et al., "Uber Is Servicing New York's Outer Boroughs More Than Taxis Are," FiveThirtyEight, August 10, 2015.

57. Matt Flemengeimer, "City Hall, in a Counterattack, Casts Uber as a Corporate Behemoth," *New York Times*, July 20, 2015.

58. Gregory Ferenstein, "Poll: New Yorkers Overwhelmingly Oppose Uber Regulations," *Forbes*, July 22, 2015.

59. Emma G. Fitzsimmons and William Neuman, "This Time It's Uber on the Defensive in Battle with New York," *New York Times*, July 27, 2018; and Emma G. Fitzsimmons and Noam Scheiber, "New York City Considers New Pay Rules for Uber Drivers," *New York Times*, July 2, 2018.

60. Fitzsimmons and Neuman, 2018.

61. Fitzsimmons and Neuman, 2018.

62. Fitzsimmons and Neuman, 2018.

63. Fitzsimmons and Neuman, 2018.

64. Fitzsimmons and Neuman, 2018.

65. Paresh Dave, David Pierson, and Makeda Easter, "Uber's Scandals Test the Patience of Investors—and the Public," *Los Angeles Times*, June 12, 2017.

66. Zoe Kleinman, "Uber: The Scandals That Drove Travis Kalanick Out," BBC, June 21 2017.

67. Casey Newton, "This Is Uber's Playbook for Sabotaging Lyft," *The Verge*, August 26, 2014.

68. Sasha Lekach, "NYC Caps Number of Ubers and Lyfts in the Streets and Gives Drivers Higher Hourly Rate," *Mashable*, August 8, 2018.

69. Dana Rubinstein, "Uber and Lyft Stop Accepting New Drivers in New York City," *Politico*, April 29, 2019.

70. Rubenstein, "Uber and Lyft."

71. Edward Ongweso, "The Lockout: Why Uber Drivers in NYC Are Sleeping in Their Cars," *Vice Motherboard*, March 19, 2020.

Chapter 6

1. This brief biographical sketch of Gutenberg is taken from Margaret Leslie Davis, *The Lost Gutenberg: The Astounding Story of One Book's Five-Hundred-Year Odyssey* (New York: TarcherPerigee, 2019), p. 17.

2. The quotation is attributed to Elizabeth Eisenstein. See Niall Ferguson, *The Square and the Tower: Networks and Power, from the Freemasons to Facebook* (New York: Penguin Press, 2018), p. 83.

3. On the diffusion of the printing press in Europe, see Ferguson, *The Square and the Tower*, p. 82.

4. For a comprehensive quantitative analysis of the role of the printing press in spreading Reformation laws throughout Germany, see Jeremiah Dittmar and Skipper Seabold, "New Media and Competition: Printing and Europe's Transformation after Gutenberg," *Journal of Political Economy* (conditionally accepted).

5. Mark Aguiar et al., "Leisure Luxuries and the Labor Supply of Young Men," *Journal of Political Economy* 129, no. 2 (2021): 337–647.

6. Jeremy Greenwood et al., "Technology and the Changing Family: A Unified Model of Marriage, Divorce, Educational Attainment, and Married Female Labor-Force Participation," *American Economic Journal: Macroeconomics* 8, no. 1 (2016): 1–41.

7. The search on Reddit was conducted on June 9, 2023.

8. Laurel Wheeler et al., "LinkedIn(to) Job Opportunities: Experimental Evidence from Job Readiness Training," *American Economic Journal: Applied Economics* 14, no. 2 (2022): 101–25.

9. See Martin Gurri, *The Revolt of the Public and the Crisis of Authority in the New Millennium* (San Francisco: Stripe Press, 2018).

10. Krystal Hu, "ChatGPT Sets Record for Fastest-Growing User Base—Analyst Note," Reuters, February 2, 2023.

Conclusion

1. Francis Bacon, *The Essays or Counsels, Civil and Moral, of Francis Ld. Verulam Viscount St. Albans* (Mount Vernon, NY: Peter Pauper Press, 1970), p. 196.

2. John T. Dalton and Andrew J. Logan, "A Vision for a Dynamic World: Reading *Capitalism, Socialism and Democracy* for Today," *Independent Review* 24, no. 4 (2020): 567–77.

Index

Note: Information in figures is indicated by *f*; n designates a numbered note.

About the Authors

John T. Dalton is an associate professor of economics at Wake Forest University in Winston-Salem, North Carolina. His areas of expertise include international trade, growth and development, macroeconomics, economic history, and the life and economics of Joseph Schumpeter. He has been published in leading peer-reviewed journals, including the *Journal of International Economics*, *Economic Development and Cultural Change*, *Macroeconomic Dynamics*, *Southern Economic Journal*, the *Journal of Economic Education*, and other peer-reviewed journals. Dalton has been a visiting scholar at the Kiel Institute for the World Economy, the Chinese University of Hong Kong, and the Institute for Empirical Macroeconomics at the Federal Reserve Bank of Minneapolis. He has presented his work at seminars and conferences and in public talks around the world. He first encountered Schumpeter as a teenage reader of *Capitalism, Socialism and Democracy* and has been wrestling with the ideas of that book ever since.

Andrew J. Logan is a corporate strategy manager at Anduril Industries, a technology startup focused on bringing disruptive commercial products to the U.S. Department of Defense. Previously, Logan was at McKinsey & Company, where he focused on innovation and emerging technologies in the defense industry, and at the Federal Reserve Bank of Chicago, where he worked in the Macroeconomic Research division. With a deep interest in the life and economics of Joseph Schumpeter, Logan has coauthored four academic articles on the subject, which appeared in the *Journal of Economic Education*, the *Independent Review*, the *Review of Austrian Economics*, and the *International Review of Economics Education*. Logan first encountered Schumpeter in one of John Dalton's classes and, profoundly influenced both by Schumpeter's writings and John's excellent teaching, has sought to bring creative destruction to life in his professional career.

Libertarianism.org

Liberty. It's a simple idea and the linchpin of a complex system of values and practices: justice, prosperity, responsibility, toleration, cooperation, and peace. Many people believe that liberty is the core political value of modern civilization itself, the one that gives substance and form to all the other values of social life. They're called libertarians.

Libertarianism.org is the Cato Institute's treasury of resources about the theory and history of liberty. The book you're holding is a small part of what Libertarianism.org has to offer. In addition to hosting classic texts by historical libertarian figures and original articles from modern-day thinkers, Libertarianism.org publishes podcasts, videos, online introductory courses, and books on a variety of topics within the libertarian tradition.

Printed in the USA
CPSIA information can be obtained
at www.ICGtesting.com
JSHW080751230624
65158JS00004B/10